TINY HOMES

The Step-by-step Guide to Shipping Tiny House

(The Ultimate Easy Guide to Discover How to Building Your Dream Home)

Laura Pennell

Published By John Kembrey

Laura Pennell

All Rights Reserved

Tiny Homes: The Step-by-step Guide to Shipping Tiny House (The Ultimate Easy Guide to Discover How to Building Your Dream Home)

ISBN 978-1-77485-344-3

All rights reserved. No part of this guide may be reproduced in any form without permission in writing from the publisher except in the case of brief quotations embodied in critical articles or reviews.

Legal & Disclaimer

The information contained in this book is not designed to replace or take the place of any form of medicine or professional medical advice. The information in this book has been provided for educational and entertainment purposes only.

The information contained in this book has been compiled from sources deemed reliable, and it is accurate to the best of the Author's knowledge; however, the Author cannot guarantee its accuracy and validity and cannot be held liable for any errors or omissions. Changes are periodically made to this book. You must consult your doctor or get professional medical advice before using any of the suggested remedies, techniques, or information in this book.

Upon using the information contained in this book, you agree to hold harmless the Author from and against any damages, costs, and expenses, including any legal fees potentially resulting from the application of any of the information provided by this guide. This disclaimer applies to any damages or injury caused by the use and application, whether directly or indirectly, of any advice or information presented, whether for breach of contract, tort, negligence, personal injury, criminal intent, or under any other cause of action.

You agree to accept all risks of using the information presented inside this book. You need to consult a professional medical practitioner in order to ensure you are both able and healthy enough to participate in this program.

TABLE OF CONTENTS

INTRODUCTION 1

CHAPTER 1: MOBILE HOMES 4

CHAPTER 2: DESIGN TRICKS FOR YOUR TINY HOME 12

CHAPTER 3: WHAT'S THE REASON TO SHOULD YOU MOVE TO A TINY HOUSE? 20

CHAPTER 4: ASPECTS TO BE AWARE OF WHEN CHOOSING TO BUILD A SMALL HOUSE 26

CHAPTER 5: THE TINY HOUSE MOVEMENT 38

CHAPTER 6: THE BUILDING PROCESS IN YOUR TINY HOUSE 45

CHAPTER 7: THE PROS AND CONS OF TINY HOUSE LIVING 54

CHAPTER 8: SMALL HOUSE FURNISHING 58

CHAPTER 9: DECORATING, AND FILLING YOUR TINY HOUSE 70

CHAPTER 10: PARKING YOUR TINY HOUSE 82

CHAPTER 11: PARKING TINY HOUSES 87

- CHAPTER 12: GET GREEN AND OFF THE GRID 97
- CHAPTER 13: WHAT TO BUILD A TINY HOUSE USING THE BUILDING STAGES 104
- CHAPTER 14: RENOVATE, REORGANIZE AND CELEBRATE! 119
- CHAPTER 15: DECIDING TO LIVING IN A SMALL HOUSE . 126
- CHAPTER 16: THE CHANGES IN LIFESTYLE: HOW TO DEAL WITH IT 135
- CHAPTER 17: EASIEST HOME ORGANIZATION HACKS 142
- CHAPTER 18: DIFFERENT TYPES OF TINY HOUSES. 166
- CHAPTER 19: THE BENEFITS OF TINY HOUSES 172
- CHAPTER 20: TINY HOUSE DESIGN ESSENTIALS - INTERIOR 177
- CONCLUSION 182

Introduction

A movement of social justice known as "Tiny Living" has swept all over the world, generating an interest among those who are considering reshaping their lives. The movement is encouraging people to take a look at the way they live and to make drastic changes.

At the heart of this movement is the downsizing of living spaces, transforming them from traditional dwellings to tiny dwellings. Other aspects of living in tiny homes include self-sufficiency, establishing financially sound plans for the future, life simplifying, and environmental awareness.

The typical American household size has been constant through the years. However, the space required for a comfortable life has dramatically grown.

This has had a significant economic impact because many of these homes were bought with loans.

There are environmental issues that come with living in luxurious homes. There is an increase in energy demand as well as the carbon footprint that is left behind is now catastrophic.

This book provides information to assist you to determine if living in a small house is an option that will benefit you. The following subjects are covered:

* What exactly is an Tiny House?

*The History of the Tiny House or Tiny Living Movement

* Why Should You Move into the Tiny House?

* The Advantages of Living in a Small House

Things to Consider prior to making a decision

* Top 10 Tips for Moving to the Tiny House

* How to Adjust To Your Tiny House

Chapter 1: Mobile Homes

According to the sounds"mobile home" means the dwelling space that one can take anyplace. A lot of Americans especially those who reside below the typical income, live in various kinds and styles of mobile home. Mobile homes come in a variety of dimensions and shapes, with the majority are made up of huge cargo. Any dwelling that is the average size of 400 sq metres or less will make it a less difficult burden to tow during the long distance. There are many kinds that are tiny (small) mobil homes that are in use to be in use today:

Boats

A boat may appear to be a totally bizarre idea for a typical homeowner, especially for those who have lived in a typical suburb for at least three generations. But the practice of living by water has been in existence since the time of discovery for seafaring. Since the end of the medieval period and especially in the Age of Exploration in the mid-15th Century sailors who traveled across continents have been used to living on galleons as well as frigates that cruised across oceans for many months. Modern sailors are unable to feel the distinction of living either on the land and in the sea.

There are a few with an enthralling spirit, who cannot avoid the lure the water. For them who are secluded, the compact and flat surface was strange. So, a floating home is likely to draw a large number of admirers.

Nowadays living aboard boats is convenient for those whose income is only dependent on the ocean or river. Fishermen who are unable to finance the mortgage on an entire lot or house, or a flat property could simply furnish their lifeline vehicles with sufficient space to live in. Similar is the case for academics such as marine ecologists and fluvial ecologists and even those who hunt wildlife on the bounty of bayous and swamps.

A lot of low-income families in Asian countries that sell or trade their goods in rural communities reside in floating homes, one of the communities that are known for their extravagant and lavish scenery often featured on travel magazines. In Europe the living on boats is more an aesthetic choice than a actual necessity. Netherlands is an example. It is among the European nations with the greatest number of floating homes. Its rising levels of sea that slowly cover the low-lying Dutch terrain could increase its appeal and economic viability.

There are numerous families, not just in America but all over the world, who have customized their boat's interiors to make them more comfortable. The boats are usually three rooms , aside from the engine and utility area that keep the boat in motion. The main benefit of these kinds of homes is that electricity is provided by generators that run on fuel. This could help avoid the hassle of paying electric bills. Floating homes are connected to jetties, which homeowners typically lease for a specific time period prior to the next trip. Tieing up a boat home is about as easy like closing the garage of a normal suburban home. Anchoring boats that aren't tied is a common practice at a lower level, particularly in less shallow depths of the open ocean to prevent being swept away by the wind (or cut up at worst).

Boats are a popular choice for those who want a simple yet unique life. It is crucial to remember that maintaining of boat homes is a huge task that requires a large amount of sea-related capabilities. Today, learning these abilities is not too difficult.

Wagons

A car may appear to be a an odd object to convert into a dwelling, but living in the form of a "wheeled home" was not new concept that was developed only in the present. Since the early medieval era the gypsies of Europe (particularly their fellow Romani people of the Balkans) have earned a reputation for their erratic behavior. They are known to wander around the city's outskirts as wandering entertainers and traders who have their very own camps. In the 18th century, Americans living in the eastern portion from the 13 colonies travelled in huge numbers through to the Appalachian Mountains. In the early days in the Westward Expansion, migrants have resided in their horse-drawn wagons for weeks and were in motion, vigilant against raids by angered Native American tribes.

Today the majority of Americans might still have that similar tense spirit that inspired their pioneer predecessors. People who are missing the convenience of apartments or homes in the suburbs have a feeling of homelessness but there are others who just are "road-sick" in the event that they are unable to travel on the highways of the continent. In fact, the United States is still the most significant consumer and manufacturer of trailers and residential wagons today. However "road-sickness" might not be an exclusively American phenomenon , as other countries with people who travel certainly relate.

A wagon is the ideal tiny home for people who are constantly moving. People who prefer this type of living space are those whose lives depend on constant movement from one city or town to the next. There's a broad range of professions that meet this definition, however everyone would consider the purchase of a house (plus the huge mortgage that is entailed by it) extremely unpractical when they're in active service.

Wagons comprise the majority percent of mobile homes that are classified as tiny homes. In reality, most of these houses do not exceed 400 square meters in total size. Though the main reason for the purchase of these houses built that are on wheels is the ease in moving them from spot in one place to another most significant benefit was the elimination of homesickness in the event of an in-between vacation. In reality, these wagon houses possess the greatest practical advantage when choosing rural and undeveloped areas as the destination (e.g. forests, desert or plains). They also possess an appealing aesthetic in the wild.

The majority of electricity is obtained from generators that use fuel, but some home owners will connect their main utility unit into any station which offers it at an affordable cost. The only drawback to having an automobile (van or truck) home is the price of fuel. However, some creative homeowners have found alternative ways to reduce the costs of buying fuel for both the home generator as well as the engine of the vehicle. A few of these wagons are equipped with solar panels to the outermost layer on the inside of the shell.

A home with a wagon gives residents the flexibility of moving into and out of the region at short notice. This kind of residence has many advantages due to its distinctiveness. For instance, residents are given plates that are registered as addresses. Furthermore, no landlord nor housing agent can ever issue a foreclosure in order to avoid payments of charges. America is the world's leading country with rental parking spaces for houses with wheels since the tiny home is commonplace in their ever-changing society.

Chapter 2: Design Tricks For Your Tiny Home

If you are building a small house making the most of every square inch of space is essential. Even though having less stuff around can aid by making the new house easier to manage and more comfortable to reside within, there's many ways to design your home that can be used to enhance your living experience. See them below.

1. Use your floors to your advantage.

What people often do not realize is that there's a plenty of untapped space under their feet. With floor-mounted storage units that you can store nearly every thing you own. It doesn't matter if it's a pair seasonal boots or books you can keep everything neat and tidy without taking up too much of your space. Additionally, you could also use the floor joists with small cubbies. Be aware that you shouldn't be able to carpet your floors if you utilize it as storage for your belongings.

2. Use loft beds

A bedroom without a bed is a sad and scary thought for some, but it's not as scary as it may seem. If your home is small and features high ceilings it is possible to make it a fake bedroom. There may not be wall that is enclosed for privacy but at the very least you could make use of the space over your head. Additionally, it will encourage you to get up from the bed earlier to take a look around.

3. Let natural light in your home.

If you let natural light into your home the house will appear larger from the inside. To achieve this all you have to do is to put in more skieslights or windows. Apart from improving the appearance of your house It is also the best way to lower the energy use.

4. Make sure you choose a Wet Bath

Wet baths are a kind of bathroom design concept where the toilet, sink and shower are crowded into one area. There is a sloped floor and drain in the shower to keep the whole bathroom dry even when not being used. Baths with water are easy to maintain and perfect for those who do not want the lavish McMansion-style baths.

5. Think about the outdoor space

Tiny homes are designed to attract owners to get out. If you're planning to build your dream home, be sure you include outdoors space within your design. In the beginning, you could create a terraced area to expand the area of your home. If you're a permanent resident on the property You can also learn how to grow plants and herbs for sustainable living.

6. Frame your doorway with frames

It is possible to surround your entrance with shelves and frames where you can keep books, as well as other small decorative items.

7. Think about getting fold-down furniture

Furniture pieces that fold down are the mainstays in tiny homes. These include tables, desks, beds or benches. This arrangement is perfect for furniture that you're not in use all the time. It is easy to build to build, since you'll need the slab of wood to build the bench or desk along with latching mechanisms and hinges to keep the furniture to its place.

8. Make your nails unique with your nail art

This trick doesn't concern keratin pattern present within your hands. These are the tiny, pointed metal pieces you use to build things. Make use of nails for hanging kitchen utensils and kitchenware, which will save the space on your countertop. Also, you can use wires as well as pegs to hang pictures and other ornaments.

9. Ceilings that are high

There isn't much living space when you're living in a small house. But, you can make up for it with a tall ceiling. In addition to being an extra bedroom, you could make use of the extra space to create a reading or office space (or you can combine both, in the event that it is possible). A shed or gable will certainly make your home appear more spacious. Additionally the high ceilings let you install windows that are larger permitting more light to penetrate.

10. Paint your home with gentle shades

The shades of blue baby, yellow and pink will make your home feel more cozy and inviting. But, in addition to painting your walls, you must also think about purchasing lighter-colored accessories and décor.

11. Learn to conquer and divide.

Frames and shelves that are hung on the walls are excellent spaces-savers. You can also make use of free-standing cabinets in your small home. In addition to organising your belongings they can also be used to cabinets to define borders within your home. This can be used to create a barrier between your entryway and your living space. Make sure you have enough space for your floor before you use this option.

12. Bring style and elegance to your entranceway

If you don't have enough room for an entrance closet, you can use shelves and benches instead. The majority of benches come with cubbies in which you can put up everyday items. Hooks can be put up on shelves for hanging bags, coats, and hats.

Chapter 3: What's the reason to

Should You Move to a Tiny House?

The decision to be small is made by people because of a variety of reasons. Many prefer a simpler life, while others opt because of financial reasons.

Escape from debt Cycle of Debt

Dream homes have become a aspect of American Dream. However, it has grown beyond the traditional white and red fence. The cost of building houses has gotten more expensive in recent years.

Based on The National Association of Home Builders (NAHB) the median cost of building a new home is $468,318. The cost of purchasing the land and the financing cost make up 18% of that figure. Construction costs average around

$289,415 which is more than 60 percent of figure provided by NAHB.

To finance their dream home, families are required to borrow funds that can be six times their annual income. To pay back the loan typically, they take out other loans. In the end, they're trapped in a vicious cycle of debt which makes their lives more difficult. There is the constant risk of losing their home if not able to pay their mortgages.

The living space that is spacious can increase the chance of spending too much. With plenty of space to store items that would otherwise be unnecessary families are forced to buy items they are unable to pay for. In spite of their extravagant lives 76 percent of Americans live pay to pay.

Tiny homes are the ideal alternative for some who wish to escape of the debt snare. The cost for building these homes is just $23,000. With the assistance of developers the price will at least half the cost of building the traditional home.

Controlling costs of living Cost of Living

The expense doesn't end after the home is constructed and completed. There are many other costs to take into consideration.

* The utility charges for a 2,700 square feet home can be quite costly. A typical house would include three bedrooms with three main rooms as well as two bathroom. It is estimated that the amount of power required to support that kind of living space is certain to be worth lots of dollars. In reality, cost of energy for traditional homes vary from 40 to $100.

* Public services like garbage disposal must be covered and accounted for into the costs for owning a home. Although it's not much however, it does add to the cost of keeping the house in good condition.

Families also have to purchase household items such as food items. This is a common expense which the family will have to establish an amount for. The larger pantries and storage space can lead to excessive purchasing. Although bulk purchases could result in savings but it can have negative effects. The purchase of more than is necessary can lead to more food wasted.

Household expenses are usually the last thing that is to be considered when evaluating the amount of money a family requires to survive. This is often the cause of incorrect budgeting and results in higher debts. Household operations are the costs of all activities members perform daily.

For instance, if each parent works, the expense will be able to cover the cash each parent spends for transportation to work.

The move to a smaller home means less money is spent on energy bills. It is estimated that the amount of power required for a home that is 400 square feet will be significantly lower than that required for a typical sized home.

Additionally, the majority of tiny homes are constructed to be self-sustaining, which means the management of waste. This reduces the cost of garbage disposal an ideal option for families to reduce their expenses significantly.

The ability to stop spending and begin saving

Living in tiny homes encourages families to reconsider what they think is essential. This could range from the amount of appliances they use to the amount they spend on food every week. It usually starts with the need to cut down on their appliances due to the small space available.

When families move into smaller houses, they make an inventory of everything they have and take only items they are unable to live without. If they previously owned three or four televisions the number usually decreases to one after they move into their small home.

Once they are used to living with only some luxuries and then it becomes a routine and they start to see them having to spend less. This causes an increase in debt. Families eventually being able to put aside more savings.

Ninety-nine percent of those who live the tiny lifestyle have less debt on their credit cards as the standard American. It's even more impressive 65 percent of people who live in tiny homes actually do not have any credit card debt, which is that they have saved more money for education or retirement.

Chapter 4: Aspects To Be Aware Of When Choosing To Build A Small House

There are many kinds of variables to consider in order in order to make the best choice when building a small home. The most crucial elements are:

Setting your short-term and long-term goals

Before you make an informed choice about what is most sensible about building a tiny house you must know the short and long-term objectives are. In the short-term it is important to know more deeply the reasons for why you're going Tiny.

It is determined by a variety of factors, such as the life stage that you are in currently. If you've lived in a huge home and have grown tired of it, the size, or if you want to travel further and discover a the smallest house to be convenient while you travel or you wish to stay clear of the risk of accumulating a large debt from your home mortgage or rent.

Recently, I made the decision to build a tiny house as I was moving across the from the same area and was looking to streamline my life so that I could work from anywhere. These goals led me to my short-term choice of the construction of a tiny home. The same way it is essential to show accuracy and clarity with regards to the goals you want to accomplish in the short-term.

Also, you need to set long-term goals for the usability of your tiny home. Some of your long-term objectives could include making use of the tiny home for a period of time, and then changing it into an income-generating rental property in order to make some cash from it.

That means that if your intention for building the small house is to reside in it for a few years before renting the property, it is essential to be able to stick to your budget to construct a home that is top of the line and will be used for many years to be.

Skills relevant for the construction of

After you've been able to establish your objectives in building your tiny home the following step would be to evaluate whether you have the skills that are appropriate for building. If you don't have the required skills for building there is no need to worry.

This is due to the fact that you can continue to develop these skills under the help by experts in the field. There are other, massive amount of information available via the internet and this book that will guide you through the process of learning these skills and then creating your small home.

It is vital to keep in mind that this guidebook will provide you step-by-step instructions for building your home, but not provide hands-on experience of the similar. It is highly recommended to join Habitat for humanity or go to tiny house workshops throughout the country to gain knowledge.

However, it is important to recognize that you don't necessarily need these abilities at the start, but you can begin building them over time. There is no need to put limits on yourself as you might not have the answers right now but that doesn't mean you cannot achieve it. You must be honest!

It is essential that you are honest with yourself right from the start. This will ensure that you don't put yourself in the process of building a small home to be like your peers.

In addition, if you're facing physical limitations Do not commit to building the home yourself. Even if you don't have the skills that is believed to stand any test.

keep working towards your small home dream. Partner with a designer to create a small house that is a perfect fit for your needs and your lifestyle.

Make a schedule for the construction of the tiny home.

A major and important aspects of building a home is the time. That means that if you're planning to construct a small home, you need to create a realistic timeline to guide the progression of the work and also how time it takes from beginning to the completion. That means you must to determine the length of time you'd like to be living in the tiny home you have built.

For instance, if you're planning to move like in my situation over the border to your small home one of the primary aspects you'll be asking yourself is how long that it will take until the home is finished.

These can all be accomplished by setting achievable goals for the construction process. This means you need be aware of the time you will need to wait from beginning to the end.

It is essential to bear in the mind that having a thorough knowledge of where you would like to be at and the time at which you must be there is crucial in making educated decisions. This is due to realisation that building takes considerable time and is the most important factor to a well-planned project.

Financial situation

Another important aspect of making a tiny home will be whether or not you've got the amount of cash to finish the task. That means you need know the amount of money you will need or have available to build the tiny home.

Keep in mind that, unlike buying a home, the construction process can allow you to save lots of dollars. Do your math!

That means that you will need to have funds to pay for the expense of items required for the construction process. The financial situation of the homeowner should not be the sole reason for building a home, but the skill that is used during the building process. This will ensure you get the best quality service for the money you spend.

The financial state you're in must be closely tied to your long-term and short-term goals so that any conflict-related deficit won't cause a blockage in the way of completing the idea.

Dream home

Another aspect to take into consideration when building your tiny home is that it's your dream home. That means that when you build your home in a tiny space it's quite simple to incorporate the characteristics in your ideal home to the home you're building.

A lot of people compliment me for purchasing my small home, but upon closer inspection they find out that I didn't purchase the house , but rather built the house up from scratch. This usually causes awkward silence during conversations because they believe that I've violated the rule of thumb for tiny homes.

Thus, you must be aware that many people have different goals for the tiny homes they would like to own. This is due to different family issues in culture, money, and lifestyle as well as the goals of other elements.

That means there is nobody else but you who can determine what is most important to you when building a tiny home. If you've taken the step of building your home in a tiny space, you're the first step towards realizing your ideal!

The site to build

The location to build your home is usually one of the biggest obstacles to construction for a lot of people. The primary reason is that throughout everyday life, you will encounter plenty of transitions that occur and so, choosing the right location for your needs both in the short and over the long run is crucial.

You must decide where you'd like construct your home to suit your needs and comfort. It can be on wheels if prefer to live a minimalist lifestyle and frequently is in motion and wants to build a house specifically for recreation goals.

If it's a traditional house, then the place of the house must be in line with guidelines for stick-built homes.

Family size and way of life

A lot of people live in tiny homes If you inquire with them, they'll inform that a tiny house should be adequate for the family as well as suitable to their life style. That implies that even if only have two people starting out and don't have children at the moment, building a small home that only accommodates just two of you isn't an appropriate and practical idea.

This is the most relevant situation for people who are planning to have children. If you're thinking of be a parent You must consider the amount of family members while making the tiny home.

I would suggest having around 100 square feet per person. It is important to take into consideration the fact that kids around, who are soon to grow into teenagers usually require an extra space for entertainment and ensuring your privacy is secured. A tiny home must also be appropriate to the lifestyle you have.

If you and your partner enjoy entertaining, there must be a space to permit entertainment. If one member of the family work at home, it is advisable that they have a place in which they can work until late and not cause disturbance to everyone else in the family.

The same applies to people who have pets and require the space to house their pets. Thus, you must be aware that a small house isn't really small, but it's enough for everything you want the house to do.

Utility plans: Plans

A tiny house isn't just about the house, but it also includes the surrounding area and the amenities within. Outdoor spaces like porches, decks and many more are crucial aspects to take into consideration when building your tiny home.

This is essential especially when you enjoy spending time outdoors with your family and making memories with them. There are many utilities available according to the kind of activities you enjoy and enjoy doing with your family.

A few of the aspects you should take into consideration is how you deal with wastes that come from your tiny home water, internet connection and electricity, among others.

It is often dependent on whether the small home you have is on wheels or constructed on the foundations. There are many issues associated with the availability and usage of these services. Consider the type of small house you have and the kind of utilities needed and the amount that you're willing to contribute to the purchase of these services in your small home.

Chapter 5: The Tiny House

Movement

The tiny-house movement is a burgeoning and expanding trend in the field of architecture and home design. It promotes living in homes that are 4000 square feet and less and the primary goal is to create a more simple way of life for those who adopt it.

The decision to downsize to a small house is an option for many for many different reasons. It could be a young adult's option to gain independence or for a family's strategy to ensure financial stability or a traveler's vehicle to travel the world living in a small home has been proven to offer the same level of comfort that a typical family home, and sometimes it even provides more. As tiny house enthusiasts would put it: It functions just like any average thousands-of-square-feet home, only with, obviously, a smaller floor space.

The Story of a Tiny History on Tiny Homes

Contrary to popular belief that tiny houses are trendy, they was not a new phenomenon. It's been in existence for decades, however this trend only became well-known in the last few years.

Lloyd Kahn, before many others was the first to propose the concept and practicality for living within a cramped space. In 1968, the pioneer attempted to construct geodesic domes to house his family after being inspired by Buckminster Fuller, another prominent person in the field of architecture. But he realized the type of home he was building was not practical for daily living after one year in one of these domes. Then he walked away from the idea right away and it was about this time that an fascination with tiny spaces began to emerge. The book "Shelter," which was published in 1973.

the former insurance broker who became a carpenter narrated the ways he experimented with different methods of creating new living spaces. One of these is a tiny dwelling. In 2012, the company of Lloyd Khan named"the Shelter Publications. released his book on tiny homes titled "Tiny Homes: A Simple Shelter" and in 2014 the author wrote and released another book about the topic called "Tiny Homes in Motion."

While Lloyd Khan has been a pioneer of tiny homes since the 1970s It was believed to be Sarah Susanka was the first to actually initiate the countermove toward the architectural style. With her series of books titled "The The Not-So-Big House" that was published in 1997 she was able to convince the masses to adopt this easy lifestyle by highlighting not just the advantages of small-sized houses and the positive effect of this homes on the environment as well as to the quality of life. She shined a spotlight on the importance of the way a person is living in his or her home, more than the location or the location in which they reside. As Sarah Susanka said people should also be conscious of environmental sustainability which is often pushed aside when designing houses. It was during the height of Sarah Susanka's campaign that tiny houses were given a completely new significance.

In 2005, as storm Katrina struck in the United States, Marianne Cusato started building tiny homes which were later called Katrina Cottages. They have an average size of 378 square feet and have been proved to be a useful and efficient living solution for in a disaster zone. The Katrina Cottages have received greater attention than the others they were first discovered by resort owners and realtors started to pay attention to Marianne Cusato's architectural style and the tiny house concept.

When another financial crisis struck in the United States from 2007 to the year 2010, the financial crisis which is being referred to as the tiny home trend gained attention because homeowners of large houses were forced to sell their homes due to the crisis, and tiny houses were cheaper alternatives in terms of purchase and maintenance. In addition, it was at this time that the environmental benefits of this particular kind of home were widely recognized. But, the tiny house's part in the market for real estate was not as high as the amount that was expected.

Tiny Homes Today

In the present, there are numerous news and television programs that focus on the tiny home movement as well as the lifestyle that comes with it. The most popular television shows about this particular trend include FYI's "Tiny House Nation" and the HGTV show "Tiny house builders."

This attention isn't restricted to TVs only. Social media, for instance, there's an evident increase in the way that the trend develops across various platforms, including YouTube (where tiny house-themed videos were watched more than 26 million times during 2013,) in addition to Facebook (where nearly eight hundred thousand users had "liked" pages that are related to the tiny-house movement, as well as this year). Search engines like Yahoo! have seen an increase in number of searches utilizing the term "tiny home" (which was searched for nearly 500 000 times during this same period). Builders of tiny houses and builders have also appeared on blogs and have even created personal websites that show off their work through the construction and construction of their tiny houses.

With these points (plus the never-ending confusion of real property interest, amortization taxes and amortization) The tiny home movement has proven to be a fascinating solution for a lot of people and has solved many of their issues simultaneously. And it's not yet too late to join the movement! There is nothing more to be expected but the trend will increase in size over the next few years.

Chapter 6: The Building Process in Your Tiny House

Your tiny house's design is entirely your choice regarding aesthetics and design. The only thing to take into consideration in this moment is that you're within the size that is recommended for the smallest house.

It is possible to go overboard with the style, but not general dimensions. In a sense you're allowed to do what you like, however, you must cut back at some point.

A small house could be built from many different materials, however for those who live in tiny homes wood is the material of choice. Onereason is that it's easy to move around and secondly because it has a certain character that everybody seems to love instantly.

Because you will construct a home within an established size limit the most important step of the construction process is planning the design. Keep in mind that the majority of tiny homes do not have the option of being renovated or expanded as they could go over the legal limit before they are subjected to the strict building code.

The majority of people's conception about what a small home generally falls into the category of the trailer house. This is the kind of home popularized by Tumbleweed Corporation. It's basically a residence that sits on the top of a trailer. It is intended to be transported from one location to another.

There's a reason. This kind of home doesn't meet any building code if it was to be placed on the foundation. This is why the majority of homeowners who own this kind of home consider it a mobile house. We'll talk more about the legal aspects in a subsequent chapter.

Here are the fundamental details you should know prior to building your own.

The dimensions of a small home shouldn't exceed these dimensions:

EXTERIOR

Height: 13'5"

Width 8'6" (at the wheels) 7'4" (walls)

Length: 20"

INTERRIOR

Height: 10'6"

Width: 6'8"

WEIGHT

Total weight of 10,100 pounds.

Tongue weight: 1,500 pounds.

You can construct an even smaller home than this but you aren't allowed to exceed the dimensions.

You'll need to buy the trailer first since it will form the foundation of the size you are able to build your tiny home.

The next thing to create an outline of the location each part of your tiny house will be. There are three areas that you need to consider in the beginning. They are your bathroom and bathroom, your kitchen and your bedroom. For the majority of tiny home owners their sleeping space typically takes the shape of an loft. Therefore, now you must focus on your kitchen, toilet and bath.

After you've allocated those two rooms to the appropriate spots, then you'll be able to decide on how large the living space is going to be, the location where your office is going to be located and the additional "rooms" you'd prefer to include in your tiny home. Remember that there is a lot of space and you'll have ensure that you have the right dimensions for the proper arrangement.

You can now begin building the framework you need. To ease the process and ensure that you do not be required to perform any significant lifting, you should build it over the frame of your trailer. The frame should be as strong as it is possible to be since it is the structure of your house and any flaws or weaknesses in the structure can lead to catastrophe, particularly when shifting from one location to another.

Use the most lightweight material you can get the best deal without compromising quality or strength in the product. This will be helpful when you take a weight measurement of your small home to determine if it meets the guidelines of how heavy it weighs when it is fully loaded with the things you have.

Install everything using strong connections that you could possibly make, particularly for the walls' corners and the roof connection because these are the areas which will likely to have the most stress points.

Make use of high-quality wood as often as you can in order to lessen the need to replace in the event of wear and wear and tear.

It is important to seal the interiors of your walls in order to decrease the requirement for extreme cooling or heating, and then line the interiors with a waterproof liner.

For windows and other places which require glass, you can use the tempered glass. They are the same kinds of glass used in cars and are extremely resistant to scratches, breaking and other kinds of damage. Additionally, if they break, they won't break into long pieces that could be hazardous and life-threatening. Instead, this kind of glass remains damaged for easy replacement, or breaks into small pieces that are easy to remove and then replace.

Be sure to adhere to industry standards to limit costs for the custom fit of all the materials you intend to employ.

Keep the eye on your budget and strive to stick to the limit of what you're able to manage to. That means that you'll need to be careful with your spending but not to the point where you'll be able to cut costs and compromise on the high-end products that you buy. Keep in mind that you're going stay in this home for quite a while and purchasing materials that aren't suitable for the task will cost you more in the end to repair and replace. Be sure to budget enough to remain within budget but not go too far.

Although all of these are in progress, you might be looking for a suitable piece of land on which you can build your tiny home (if you're not set to treat it as trailer home and transporting it from one location in the same area to another). There are many websites to explore as well as ask locals for recommendations and generally network as far as you can in order you can locate the property that allows you to fulfill your dream to live in a less typical house, away from the daily hassles of urban lifestyle.

Your top priority right now is land that you can purchase (if you're looking for a long-term solution) or rent (if you only plan to live there for a short period) as well as trade (you'll need to purchase the land before you sell it).

The term "tiny" house has grown to include homes which aren't mobile but only a little larger in size than an mobile home. These are the tiny homes that are found on the streets of New York, France, Germany and many other countries in which people have converted a small space into a fully-sized tiny home.

There are plenty of inspiration sources to help you think through and build your home. Look around for ideas prior to choosing a style that you love. You must be sure you like the plans you create because tiny homes do not give you a lot of customization options. After you've constructed it, it'll remain as it is for the duration of its existence. The only way to make improvements is to make a few adjustments or start with a tiny new house further down the road.

If you're blessed with the funds you can build your home in a protected area so that you can minimize exposure to elements during the construction phase. This is it for now, take out your saw and hammer and begin cutting and pounding some nails.

Chapter 7: The Pros And Cons of

Tiny House Living

Being in the midst of a small space isn't just about the great things, it's also about taking a look the advantages and disadvantages. Here's what you need to be aware of...

Pros

Tiny homes can last for a lifetime! If constructed properly and no matter for whom they are for--whether it's an entire family, a couple or just one individual, a tiny home will last many years, and be more like a home contrasted to huge mansions, with some areas of which you don't even utilize.

You can save even more. According to studies, 80 percent of students start work and then spend the remaining years of their lives approximately $40,000-$60,000 in debt, mostly because they've been spending the majority of their money trying to construct or purchase homes that might be taken away in the event that mortgage payments aren't made. Through the use of a small house, you reduce the amount you otherwise have used to pay for mortgages, and will have more cash to assist you in navigating your life without stress.

It's not too difficult to get used to. Once you've mastered the art of it, you'll discover that you feel at your home. This is due to the fact that it's yours because you've constructed it from scratch and there are a few facets of your own personality as opposed to a home that was probably used by others during the time.

It addresses issues for seniors. The United States has RV parks throughout all over the United States that host seniors and veterans, as well as those without homes. It gives them the freedom to live their lives without having to feel like they are required to constantly accept other people's desires. This gives them the chance to spend their last days in style!

It allows you to live green. It won't create too many carbon emissions; you can make use of recycled materials, or choose solar power - the options are limitless.

It's a great way to start a home! In case you're still contemplating building your dream home in the near future it is possible to use tiny homes to build your initial home. It should be a place that allows you to allow your dreams to expand; where you can let yourself save moneyand pursue your desires. One day you'll thank yourself for it.

Cons

What is the best place to build your tiny home? Do you have any information about RV parks? Does your zoning zone work for your house? Are you able to use it in the area you live in?

What kind of home is it? It could be a tiny house that is grounded to the ground, or is it an apartment that is mobile? Would you choose to go with minimalist design in a way that you can remain in one spot filled with everything you require, or would you prefer to take your home to wherever you go?

How big is your family? You must ensure that the home you choose to live in will meet your requirements.

What's your life style? Do you think that you'll be able to live this type of lifestyle or do you continue to search for something more?

Chapter 8: Small House Furnishing

When you are moving into your home should ensure that it's well-furnished. This is essential since it can bring vitality into your living space. These are essential tips for furnishing your home in a small space:

Decoration

The design of a small house will help to make your home appear bigger and more attractive to your guests and you. If you're decorating your small home the best method in making it seem large is to utilize soft pastel hues to your design. This can create a warmer atmosphere and make the home more welcoming. Additionally, think about using colors to boost your mood while in your small home.

In general, a smaller home must be clean and clear of clutter. Utilize every inch of space by constructing cabinets for storage in your walls to ensure you have enough room to keep your possessions in a neat and organized fashion. Consider floating shelves to ensure that you make the most of the space you have.

Enhance the flow of sunlight into your small home by using a basic window treatment. If you have windows, opt for curtains that can be pulled away from the window to let sunlight in, or opt for blinds that roll and Roman blinds. Additionally, think about the use of full length curtains since they can create the illusion of space by drawing the eyes towards the sky. In addition, using stripes for your curtains can enhance the look of space. Consider adding well set out furniture and big wall mirrors to your layout to add some the perfect balance to your small home.

Furniture

If you have a small space, choosing the right furniture could make the difference between your home feeling spacious or comfortable. Here are some furniture options that you can look at for your small home:

Pedestal table

This is a round table that has a pedestal base that will easily be incorporated into your living room. Because it is a round table, it is not a problem working with sharp edges. Additionally, you can use the table to seat more people at the table.

Stools in a stack.

This furniture is ideal for when you're hosting guests. A stool set does take up little space and can be easily put away inside a room until guests arrive to take them out for use.

Small armchairs.

For your table with a small pedestal, think about having armchairs are easy to stack when not being used. This will allow you to efficiently make the most of space in your home because you will only take off the comfy armchairs only whenever you require them.

A small table to personalize

If you are working from a small home, you'll require a table that will allow you to complete the job efficiently. If you're working on laptops and your table requirements for office use are not too complicated, you can think of something different and think about an adjustable desk that can be set up whenever you are working and then fold it in half and store it away when it's time to move on to other tasks. This will to free up the floor space and help improve the appearance of your home. well-organized.

Beds with multiple functions

The majority of people sleep for a portion of the day. You can make the most of the space that your mattress takes up by getting an all-purpose bed. For instance, you can use a bed that doubles as an actual bed as well as a sofa to fold it down and use it as a seating area during the day time, particularly when you're having more guests or need to be comfortable and enjoy a night of art, you can could use it as an extra bed.

Folding dining table

It's another fantastic furniture piece that will make a huge difference to your space.

Since you eat only three times per daily, having a folding dining table is an excellent idea for a small home. It requires less space, and is used only for a couple of times per day and can keep your tiny home appearing spacious throughout the day.

Appliances

You've worked for what seems like endless weeks laying out the foundations of your tiny home framing, roofing, trimming, sheathing and insulate your tiny home. You have finally achieved your the goal of building your very own home and are now at the point of furnishing your house. What small home appliances would be the best to choose? Which ones are best suited to the requirements of your tiny living space the most effectively?

Apart from furniture, you will require several devices to help make the small home more comfortable. These are the most essential appliances to consider in your move to a tiny house:

Small Flat Screen TV

You will require some type of entertainment for your small home. Television is a common feature in many homes, and having it can bring entertainment for your small home. A small flat-screen TV will let play music or view films, and be aware about the world around you , while also making space. The fact that you have a TV does not necessarily mean you'll pay lots in money for cable television There are many entertaining shows of the public channels. This can save you lots of money. If saving money isn't your primary concern, then consider a laptop to watch videos online or streaming news, as well as other TV shows via the internet.

Refrigerators

The options for small home appliances including fridges are numerous and deciding the best one to invest your hard-earned cash into could be a daunting task, therefore let's examine the different aspects to take into consideration before making a decision. The first thing you should consider is your electrical source and if the small home is connected to a grid or run by an solar power system. Contrary to what a most people believe fridges actually pose an enormous burden on the solar system, and consume approximately 1 kWh each day (350 annually) in the case of one 18 c.f. unit.

The second consideration is estimation of the size of the refrigerator and determining the number of cubic feet is sufficient to meet your needs. We've all been taught that larger units are preferable, however it happens more often, it ends full of food spoilage as we accumulate more than we require in it. However, a refrigerator that isn't big enough could become frustration, particularly when you are unable to store enough food to meet your requirements.

Another consideration is your lifestyle, budget and your personal preferences. There's a wide range of options available to meet your requirements. Therefore, spend some time studying the market and choose the perfect refrigerator that meets your requirements while saving space in your small home.

Ranges and Ovens

Different options are available with regard to cooking surfaces, and which one you select is contingent the heating source is (electric or propane) as well as the amount of people you cook for, as well as the space you'll have to spare for ovens or a range.

In deciding the right unit it is essential to be open and honest regarding what your actual needs are. If you are able, go to or lease a property on AirBnB or any other site with a range that is similar to the one you're contemplating and see if it meets your specific requirements. You might be surprised by how small a kitchen can make a difference in the preparation of even a big meal

One of the most important aspects to consider when selecting the selection or more to purchase is

The source of heart (electricity or Propane)

This decision is based on whether you're linked to the grid or make use of solar panels. Cookers and ranges that require electricity are a significant load on your energy source, and unless you have access to an reliable grid, I'd advise you to choose propane appliances. This means that if you are planning to travel around your tiny house more frequently it is best to opt for propane-powered appliances.

The dimension of the range, or oven

The size of your kitchen appliance is another important aspect in deciding of what to purchase. The size of the appliance also reflects the total floor space of your house. If you live in a home that is smaller than 400 square feet, then you'll require a smaller oven or range than if your house is larger than 500 sq. feet. If you eat outside the majority often, smaller kitchen appliances are the best choice for you those who cook primarily at home.

Dishwashers

Many who are devoted to minimalist living prefer to wash dishes using hands to reduce space and costs by not investing in dishwashers. However, not all people are an advocate of washing dishes by hands. If you are in this category, then dishwashers is the ideal chance. There are plenty of small to medium-sized dishwashers that are able to fit in the tiny space of your home and still leave plenty of room. For instance, drawer-style dishwashers have a low profile and provide a lot of assistance when it comes to washing small quantities of glass, dishes and even glasses.

Chapter 9: Decorating, and Filling

Your Tiny House

After you've bought or constructed your small home You don't want it to become an empty structure. You'll want to carry all the things that you require to enjoy an enjoyable, satisfying experience. Due to the small amount of space it is possible that you don't be able to decorate or fill up your tiny home with the items you need. This article will help you understand exactly how to decorate and fill your small home.

Kitchen stocking:

A minimalist kitchen should make the perfect first move in filling your home with essentials for survival. These are the things that I had in my kitchen, but keep in mind it is important to note that your "essential essential items" list is different for every person. The first thing you should ask yourself is this "If you're planning to buy the house you've always wanted then what are the essential items for the beginning days?"

Iron skillet Iron skillet - It is one of my favorite kitchen appliances. You can cook up some wings of chicken or bake brownies using it. Iron skillets serve multiple functions. They can be used to transfer into the oven when you have for switching between stovetop as well as the oven.

Stock pot that has lid If you plan to steam or boil all of your food items using a stockpot with lid is essential. You can prepare soups pasta, sauces, and other dishes and use it to fry or soak your food.

Good knife set - Look for an item that is robust and doesn't quickly go dull. If you're on the edge or in a mobile home it is important for your kitchen appliances to last. While this is my personal opinion, a quality knife set must come with warranty and offer the possibility of going to a professional sharpener.

Cutting board - Once again it is purely an individual choice however, I prefer an acrylic cut-board to ensure that my knives won't scratch the counter-tops within my tiny home.

Spatula - If you are using an iron cookware, it is important to be in a position to sear and flip your food. A spatula will assist greatly in that.

Kettle - If your needs are hot water then a kettle is an excellent kitchen gadget to possess. Maybe you're planning prepare coffee or require it to make tea.

Plates/bowls - I'm aware many people eat from their stock pots, however I prefer having plates or bowls to keep my food in. Buy a plate or a bowl made of of plastic, as it won't be broken if you dropped it upon the flooring. I'm not talking about ceramic bowls or plates made of paper that are only used once but a more durable one that lasts.

Utensils It's an obvious one. If you don't plan on eating all of your food with your hands having a few kitchen Utensils on hand is a must. You should have a couple of forks, or one or two spoons and you'll be set.

Decorate your home

In a study conducted in 2009 with the Barnard Retail Consulting Group of Upper Montclair, Americans spend an astounding $343 billion on home improvement. Talk about a massive shopping outing!

Because your home will be a small home, many of the trends used by people in normal homes (i.e. huge tabletops, futons) aren't applicable to your situation. In a tiny home and a small space, you will not only need to squeeze every need within a limited space and you'll be required to ensure that the space is functional and not too crowded otherwise you'll be an extremely uncomfortable experience. Here are some tips for getting the most of your smaller space while still retaining an abundance of style:

Make use of multi-purpose furniture when you are trying to install furniture in a small home there isn't enough space for single-purpose furniture. This is where multi-purpose furniture comes in. For instance, a sofa can be converted into bed. A desk chair could be transformed into a dining chair well. A separate Desktop monitor could be used as a TV set. Walls is a great place for storage of kitchen tools. Get creative! There are always ways to decrease your space you need to use.

Paintings and posters - I'm sure there's still room on your wall to embellish with paintings and posters. My personal view, but the most important thing is to avoid overdoing it. Set up one or two paintings or posters. This will make your small walls appear well-lit, but not over decorated.

Hanging storage space above the bed you could have a basket for laundry hanging from the ceiling's top. Imagine this. You're in the shower and you're required to grab your shower towel and your clothes. Usually, you need to move across the room to grab towels or your clothes However, with a hanger space it is easy to reach up and over for everything you require.

SentrySafe Fireproof chests - Everyone has valuables. Some people keep it under their mattresses (not recommended) Some people also own wall-mounted safes and other individuals have locked wall cabinets. If you live in a small house isn't there any way that you'll be able to dedicate six square feet for a safe. Get the SentrySafe Fire Chest so that you are able to protect your important documents and valuable possessions.

Entryway coat hanger and organizers - As you walk into your home you will find several coat hooks and a shelf you can put your things on. This could be a space to store photos, notes or even letters for postal services. It also serves as an excellent reminder for you. Additionally, these items will allow you to create an inviting image when you have guests at your home.

Space for books If you're like me, you'll never need room for your books because the majority of my publications are electronic copies. If you're a book lover you want to keep, don't make a separate shelf (especially when it's not multi-purposed). Instead, you could create an over-the-door shelf by nailing an ledger board to the header, and then screw the shelf board onto the ledger and put in a few 90 degree brackets.

Bags for luggage - Instead of needing to build the closet which will eat the space, consider using luggage bags to store your clothes. Yes, they may not seem more "fashionable" for your small home's decor however, they are enormous space savers.

Do your best to digitally digitize as many items as you can. If you're not a fan of the digital revolution, you're free to ignore this. However, digitizing books photos, and even papers could be a great space-saver. Instead of setting up an book shelf or creating numerous photo album, you can use flash drives as well as an external drive.

Beds that are wall mounted Imagine having the bed you want to simply flip over and put on the wall when it is not being used. It can be a wonderful space-saving device.

Storage underneath the staircase If you're planning to have multiple floors in your small home, you should think about creating an area of storage under your staircase. For example, you could have drawers under your staircase.

The best way to think vertically is to think about the interior of your house from a vertical perspective, instead of horizontally. If you aren't able to spread it out and spread out, you can reach upwards. If you're struggling with verticality you can purchase an adjustable step stool that folds, and place items you don't need as often on top.

Safety Checks

Security should be your primary first priority, no matter if you live in a tiny dwelling or not. When I was designing my tiny home, there were certain aspects that seemed unsafe. For example, I thought to myself thisquestion "Will my windows have to be size to be utilized to escape, too?" And of course the answer was not. The incident made me think of other methods to ensure my home is secure. I began writing some ideas down, which eventually became the form of a list.

Check for safety in the sleeping area:

Make sure that the electrical cords aren't tied or stapled to the ground.

Set up a window to be used as an escape plan in the event of an emergency

Make sure that the extension cords have been properly calibrated to carry the correct amount of electricity they will be carrying.

Check that an alarm for smoke is installed and functioning properly

Do not place ladders or other equipment to loft space in an area that is in direct traffic

Check for safety in the bathroom and kitchen

Electrical appliances should not be plugged in when they are not being used.

Electrical appliances that are plugged in pose dangers due to the water source that is nearby in your kitchen or bathroom (especially applicable in smaller homes because there is a distance of source of water to the electrical appliance smaller)

Be sure to keep cords of appliances far from surfaces that are hot (like ovens and stove tops)

Don't leave your electrical heaters or hot plates unattended while they are on and used.

In bathrooms and kitchens be sure the outlets you have installed are replaced by Ground Fault Circuit Interruptors.

Check for fire safety

Create an emergency escape plan in the event of a fire. Make a list of escape routes if you're in different areas within the tiny home.

Make sure your vent pipe is well-maintained and clean.

Make sure you keep your incense clear of sheets and blankets, or other kinds of fabric

Inflammable liquids such as paint and propane, should be stored safely away from sources of heat.

Install a certified fire extinguisher within your house.

Carbon monoxide is a poisonous gas that can be detected by a safety check:

Be careful when using any type of fuel (gas or wood, oil coal, kerosene or coal) inside your home. This is particularly true for those living in tiny homes as the area is smaller. The burning of fuel in the indoors can cause suffocation often in smaller spaces.

Never use a charcoal barbecue in the house.

Set up a CO detector next to the smoke detector

Chapter 10: Parking Your Tiny House

Another problem you'll have to face is parking your tiny home. You want to be free of mortgages, and to have less clutter within your home. But, what's going to happen if require a parking spot for your tiny mobile home? Can you find a place? Is your tiny home accepted? There are unfortunately increasing restrictions every year when it comes the parking of your small home in specific areas.

Tiny House Communities

Certain cities in the USA are beginning tiny houses communities. Lyons, Colorado and Portland, Oregon are two places where tiny house communities are being built. A few RV park in California permit tiny house constructions.

The challenge is to determine whether the communities are secure. Do they offer a safe environment in which you'd like to raise your children? Similar to the RV park and other manufactured homes, you're likely to see all sorts of people within the region. It is important to conduct your research to make sure you're choosing a safe location to park during your travels.

There aren't all communities that claim to offer "free" park. There is a chance that charges are the same as those in RV parks. The rental charges will be addressed in the future in greater specific detail.

RV Park

In the past couple of years RV parks have changed their opinions on what they will allow you to park your tiny home. Similar to many other communities, those living in RV parks are now deciding that tiny homes aren't similar to RVs, and are too large to fit in the RV parks. It could be that RV parks aren't easy to locate with reasonable prices and RV owners do not wish to have their spaces taken. If you do not ask at each place, the reason you could be refused remains unclear. It is well-known the fact that RV parks are definitely becoming more strict. This makes it more difficult to find places for parking, which isn't on areas that family members and friends might permit you to park when you're within the vicinity.

Boondocking

Boondocking is a term used in RV that refers to the practice of staying on land owned by someone else or locating "free" terrain. Land that is public and does not need a fee to be an area for camping however, it allows camping. is an excellent method of traveling. Unfortunately there are a few boondocking locations in America. USA there aren't many boondocking spots accessible. The ones that are offered are usually private however, they are available to you in exchange for the payment of a small amount. Boondocking communities exist as well as websites that allow you to locate accommodation.

Rent

Locations that are public that have campsites, RV sites or parking for tiny homes generally have fees for rental of the site. They can cost as high as the amount of a mortgage. Some places cost more than $700 for parking for the duration of a month.

It will not make you in any more position to pay a premium for a spot rental for a month, as long as you pay an amount equivalent to site rental that you pay for an mortgage on an $150,000 house.

It is true that it appears negative when you read this report. But, do not get discouraged. There are people and communities that make small-sized living feasible. The trick is to do your homework and finding places for parking, based on your travel preferences. You must enter your the tiny home with your eyes wide open. The most important rule of this section is to not think that you'll always be in a position to park. RVs are usually able to be able to park at truck stops, or in certain parking spaces for retail stores however a small house is more obvious. It is necessary to obtain permission to park if the property is owned by a different. Keep in mind that your research is crucial to make living in a tiny house an accomplishment by analyzing your travel habits.

Parking for your Tiny House Steps

Create a schedule for your excursion.

Buy subscriptions to AAA boondocking websites or RV campgrounds.

Look for tiny-house communities along the way.

Consider the potential locations for parking along your route.

Check availability in advance and requirements for booking.

Create parking options along the route before leaving for your trip.

Chapter 11: Parking Tiny Houses

"Where do I locate the best place for my tiny home to be parked?" is a common query that is asked by a majority of people. But, those into this category need to worry less as this chapter will answer the question in a way that is appropriate.

Even though your house may be small, it doesn't mean you shouldn't park it wherever. It is important to take into consideration certain aspects. Obviously, where to live is the main problem that leads many peopleto avoid small houses. It's an expense for a small amount of security. It's the "grey space" that you've encountered a large number of small-sized home owners enjoying themselves in, to live the best lifestyle.

Legalities

Legal bodies have a unique perspective on tiny houses. At present, there is no definition of 'tiny home or 'tiny house' in the zoning codes. These are classified either as mobile houses, or RVs (though the classifications vary based on the area of. If a semi-trailer is a utility trailer, they're classified as 'neatly stacked loads'. However, the trailers require different permitting/registration fees and can't be occupied legally. A large majority of tiny homes fall under the RV's category. The building department is not able to interfere with them in any particular area because these are vehicles. Registration and licensing is conducted within the department of transportation. In addition, it is essential to do some structural analysis before making tiny homes. This greatly reduces the adolescent substandard construction methods that most people employ.

Mobile Home

In the event that you've registered your tiny house as a mobile home there aren't any restrictions to living full-time within mobile homes parks, or in zones that don't limit mobile homes, like downtown districts, which are legally. Though there is some flexibility, many mobile home parks adhere to parking regulations that only permit mobile homes that have been constructed by licensed and professional manufacturers. Therefore the restriction is up to your builder. This can be a thorny aspect, especially for those who are building their own tiny homes. If the path is a good idea for you, it's suggested to speak with potential places prior to commencing the building. In general, aside from taxes, this choice comes with more fees for registration and permits.

RV

You are able to live in any RV park legal in the event that you're registered as an RV. Similar to mobile houses, the requirement of a manufacturer that is licensed applies to this; the majority of RV parks will allow "current RVs" that are constructed by certified manufacturers. This has resulted in the majority of small-sized home builders becoming licensed, so that they can belong to the 'certified manufacturers category. If you've chosen to follow this path be sure to only deal with manufacturers that are certified. If you're a DIY home builder having an individual certification likely impossible.

Other Options

The semi trailers as well as the 'nicely loaded load' do not allow for occupancy that is legal regardless of where they are located.

The 'Grey Zone'

The "grey zone" is the next choice for those who prefer to live in tiny houses but aren't keen on mobile homes or RV parks. They fall into the "grey zone". If you do not own a property that is yours, you might not be able live there. However, moving is simple as your home is on wheels. The best thing to do is find the perfect spot, and then live there but be aware that you might be requested to quit. This can happen, but it's not often. If you find a suitable location to park your tiny home, you should always knock on doors before even thinking about moving.

If neighbors inform them that they are not happy over neighbors who have tiny homes It's better to go away since they have a right to do so. It's not possible to disrupt their peace to'settle down'. Furthermore, with trailers, you should not have a problem moving. Before investing in tiny homes it is wise to notify everyone. Because the majority of laws against the full-time living of RVs in areas that aren't RV parks have been applied to complaints or concerns raised by neighbors. But, this doesn't mean every neighbour is "bad".

There are ways you could make neighbors more welcoming. One option is to spend an evening or two per month at the house of a neighbor (your friend) or move farther and then register your small home as mobile , as opposed to RV, etc. If your neighbor are still complaining, it's best to move on since you do not want to be in danger even in a hostile environment. It is best to talk with your neighbors prior to the visit so that you are able to know their feelings about your 'tiny home but you'll never be able to find out unless you inquire. Conversation with them might inspire them to change their views toward tiny homes.

Locating a Place

If you're looking at it from a financial standpoint It is better to purchase an existing house that includes a huge yard on which you can put your tiny home. You can then pay for your mortgage with renting the property out and live without rent. While most people utilize this as a method to avoid mortgages, it's an effective method of making sure that the debt is an instrument that improves your financial standing.

Apart from finding a home that is rented out and that earns more than the mortgage payment and has the proper arrangement, purchasing your own house has lots of advantages, including that it can be disguised. It's true that a small home can be concealed with the right home. Then, you can arrange for your tiny home to be recognized by the authorities as an ADU.

Advertisements can be placed to find a location that has RV parking. Be sure to specify the hook-ups you'll need. However, keep in mind that parking spaces may be limited due to having multiple hook-ups. For instance the 50 or 30 amp plugs can be difficult to locate compared to having two outlets of standard (15 amps).

There are some websites that offer parking spaces or land available for lease or for sale. Visit to many sites could land you with a good deal. This is advantageous for the cost and the acceptance of the small house by the neighbors. Additionally, the same message can be propagated on social media platforms like Facebook. Do your research.

But that tiny "occupier' needs to be able to monitor his own expenses and utilities and flat rates may be set for utilities , or any other amount that is suitable for both parties. If the neighbors or the host make the home unwelcoming, the 'occupier' is able to leave at will , or be asked to leave without the expense of the host or at risk. This is the risk every tiny homeowner faces when parking in a "grey space". It's a mutually beneficial scenario but letting the property owner that they need to pay on rent is the most difficult part.

Of course, you are able to buy a property bare! But, it is important to understand that you may be required to relocate in the event that you've built or parked your house in a location that is not specifically designated as a mobile or RV home even when you own the land or property.

Another option to find an appropriate settlement location for your small or tiny home is to knock on doors. Even though it's an exhausting method, it's effective. The majority of people have no idea about tiny homes or how to make a side income from leasing the land as well as renting out the smallest home. Inform land owners of the tiny home you are building and discuss hosting your tiny home and earning extra cash.

But, regardless of how attractive you make the offer appear, you must inform them of their rights and dangers involved. Talk about the amount they're willing to charge in order to have an idea of the amount you're required to be able to. A sketch or image of your house will help. sketch of your house can allow you to make your negotiations more feasible. Even though this might sound demeaning an approach to the elderly can be an excellent first step since they're the least critical when it comes to living in a small space and perhaps because they don't perceive the concept foreign as in the past the houses were small. Furthermore, the elderly may be living in a different location from their family Therefore, the thought of living who lives in the same place could provide a sense of peace and security. in addition to aiding them in running certain errands.

Chapter 12: Get Green and Off The Grid

If you are looking to drastically decrease not just your utility bills , but also your carbon footprint then you should seriously think about becoming green. There are many options to pick from. All you need to do is select those that match your needs. Here are the most popular alternatives to energy sources, as well as other green utilities that are commonly found in small homes:

Solar Panel System

A solar-powered system has become the popular alternative source of power in tiny homes, and for the right reason. It is not necessary to have lots of panels to power your home. It can supply power to your lighting and smaller appliances, like refrigerators that are low in power as well as your laptop. The tiny house owners are advised against making use of any appliance that utilizes the hot coil method since it is extremely energy-intensive. That's why when cooking, they favor gas.

A solar panel system typically includes the following components including solar panel, battery backup generator, battery bank and Volt system. You can find out more information about these components by talking to the manufacturer.

But, before you jump on the solar panel craze be sure to ensure that you have an area that you can receive the maximum light exposure on your panel. If your home is in the midst of trees, it will be difficult. If you're not sure that solar energy is suitable for your particular location You can make use of the "solar path finder" that is a device which will figure it out for you. Do some research on this tool, so that you can determine how to access it and how to utilize it.

If solar energy is appropriate for your area the following step would be to buy and set up your solar panels. The most widely used panel will provide 250 watts, so you need to decide on the number you require, based on the equipment that you'll use. Installation of the panels is fairly straightforward. Some prefer placing their panels over their roofs and others mount them on locations that get the maximum amount of sunlight. It is possible to place them on your ground instead of on top of your roof as excessive heat could actually destroy the panels.

Also, you must prepare an enclosure to house all the components that your solar panel system requires. If you're not experienced about the process of installation You should seek help from a professional so that you can install everything without damaging the investment you made.

It is highly recommended to combine the solar energy you generate with generators, especially during the winter months. Also, select the generator that has enough energy to fulfill all your requirements.

Alternative Fire Systems

If you're an outdoor enthusiast, you'll have a good understanding of the features and function of denatured Alcohol stoves. It's just as efficient as a traditional stove however, it's lightweight, affordable, produces no odor, and uses renewable energy sources. In addition it isn't explosive, and so you get the security factor also.

In order to set up an alcohol-fueled stove in your small house, you may have to locate an inexpensive, second-hand model of sailboat or RV to save cash. In other cases, you can use of the basic alcohol stoves found in most hardware stores.

Many tiny house homeowners choose to install wood stoves for two reasons to keep their homes warm, and to generate the hot water needed for bathing, as well as other needs of the home. This is possible thanks to using the "Fire Flue" system which can be installed.

Toilet Composting

If you are not averse to getting rid of a composting toilet once in a while and don't need toilet plumbing within your small home and you are looking for a composting toilet, then the composting toilet is your ideal option. It will reduce the needless water waste and, simultaneously providing your garden with organic fertilizer (just be sure to study extensively about how to make this happen).

It is suggested to buy composting toilets that separate your urine from fecal matter so that cleaning is more efficient and reduce odor. Although composting toilets are not as affordable as the classic bucket, they can reduce your time and effort as well as your health by getting it cleaned.

Make sure you check if the composting toilet you purchase is certified for health and hygiene.

Water system that is eco-friendly

Apart from the standard RV water hose connection that most tiny homeowners install, the majority also utilize two off grid system of water: rainwater capture system as well as gravity-fed water systems.

There are a variety of ways to set up rainwater collection systems, and the most popular is the most basic one. Simply install a gutter on the top of your small house to catch the rainwater, and then let it run down the pipe using a filter and then through a storage barrel. Then, you can connect a hose and spigot connected to provide your small home with water. The rainwater is a great source of water for your garden as well as to clean. It is possible to use steam distillers along with an aerator if you intend to make use of the water to wash dishes, wash the laundry, or even to cook and drink. Make sure you get the highest quality equipment and expert guidance as per your budget.

The gravity-fed system can be another method to take your small home independent of the grid and sustainable by eliminating the power-consuming water pump. It may seem like a bit complicated at first, however the construction and maintenance is very simple, especially in the event that you have an expert to set it up.

You can make your small home highly efficient and eco-friendly while using alternatives to energy sources. Together you can get the most out of nature's energy without harming it when compared to traditional homes.

Chapter 13: What to Build A Tiny House Using the Building Stages

There are numerous designs and ideas for building tiny homes. If you're looking to complete the most of it as you can within your own free time, we'll work together to give you an understanding of the what is that you really must be doing.

Planning Stage:

In the beginning, we have to consider the kind you want to build the Tiny House you are after... Do you want to build a self-sufficient tiny home that can be towed around? Or do you want to build a self-sufficient house that's not moveable?

If you are buying land or a trailer, at this point you must consider the area you would like to live in and the size your dream home will be. You might be thinking, "Well I'd like a small home that is moveable, but I'm not sure what size I want it is it?

The best way to figure this is to visit the yard of a company that makes trailers and look over the various sizes available. This will let you determine the size you want. Keep in mind the vehicle you drive in and don't purchase a trailer that you can't be able to pull.

However, if you're building an not-moveable residence, the size of your home isn't as important since you're building on the land. However, it's still essential to consider what you'll need, and how tiny you could build your home in order to be livable. This is because this isn't an ordinary-sized house We are building an extremely small home that will reduce the total cost of living.

After you have bought your land from an agency for real estate or a trailer from a reputable trailer business, you are now ready to move on to the next step.

Design stage:

With an area of land or a trailer, it is time to concentrate on the style. Making a home design is always thrilling, but it is important to collect information as well as pictures of different homes in order to have an picture of what we'd like to have. The best method for doing this is to look online by entering "Tiny houses" or searching for magazines at the local news agency or book shop.

Once you've completed the book or folder with a variety of images and styles that you'd like your tiny home to be then you can bring your home to a draftsman or an architect. A majority of people do not know about architects or draftsmen But don't fret you can just ask your builder buddies or search on the internet for a reputable professional.

After you've had your ideal Tiny House designed you are in the process of obtaining the required permits to build your dream home on a land block.

To do this, you'll be required to contact your local council to learn about the permits you are required to obtain or speak with the builder who is in your area. Since if you fail to have the right permits and construct a house where you would like, you could be paying hefty fines or having your home being taken away (if you are caught).

Foundation stage:

After you have the plans and permits for your new home then you can begin building the foundations of your house. It all is dependent on the type of house you are building either movable or non-movable.

If you're building your house on a trailer, you'll want to construct a sub-floor over the trailer to be in a position to lift your home off the trailer in case of need. This is your foundations and you'll want the subfloor to be constructed in a manner that it is able to be lifted. In this case, you can put additional bearers to permit the moving of your home.

If you want to build a non-movable home, house, you will need foundations designed specifically for the ground or soil that you intend to build your home on.

The slabs, or footings, are the foundations for what your house will sit on, so you have ensure that the foundation is stable and solid. For this, you need to have the plans which have been drawn up by an engineer, as they take into account the soil's slope and the type of foundation that is needed for the area of land upon which you'll be building your house. Sometimes, the engineer will permit two foundation types based on the soil's grade and the amount of the weight of your home is, (if it's a 3-story tiny house, you'll need higher and more sturdy foundations).

The biggest risk when you don't follow the advice of the engineer, and instead you choose the least expensive foundation. In the end, you might discover that your home is in a state of extreme deficiency and you'll have to have all the electrical, water and other layers of your house removed and rebuilt in the future.

Wall Frame Stage:

When you are at the frame stage, it is necessary to follow the guidelines that your architect has created for any structural or load bearing. However, if you want to alter the size or the dimensions of an inside wall in the future, it's okay provided that it does not take any pressure from the walls to the sides. If you are building the frame, you'll need to employ an experienced carpenter, unless you're actually a carpenter, since the frame is an essential element of your home. If you think that you can complete the task, and then you make the wrong thing, you could cause serious injury to you or your loved one. This is especially true for the house that moves since it is always moving , which could cause weakness within the building.

A tip for framing is to make sure you have at least two people working on it as you'll always require someone to supply you with the materials when you're climbing the ladder. The key to successful carpentry is to be always productively moving. If you're working on your own, you'll require three times the time than if you're working with two people. This is because of unneeded movements to get on and off ladders or trying to think of methods to lift heavy objects by yourself. In contrast, having someone else lift it alongside you, and save lots of time.

Roof stage:

After the wall frame has been constructed, we must create the roof. This will permit us to build the exterior cladding of the frame, without water damaging the material. To cover the roof of an mobile house, you'll generally require it to be Tin because it is lightweight and therefore we have to limit the the weight that we put the trailer with.

The simplest way to get the roof constructed is to buy roof trusses through a 'roof firm', and then employ carpenters to build the roof to your plans. You can purchase and place an order for this on your own if you'd like to save on materials. You just need to give the plans for your home to the truss business and they'll visit and make measurements to make sure that everything is working.

From there, you require the carpenters to install the roof battens and roofing plumbers put the roof down, and finally install the guttering.

The environmentally friendly part of your house After the roof has been completed we can purchase and install solar panels that will allow for solar panel lighting, cooling and heating. Check that your electricians already planned for this before they begin the "rough in process, as we'd like our main energy source to be derived from the solar panels. This is a significant expense at first, but we'll make the entire amount back within the first three years of owning our home.

Stage of external cladding:

It is time to organize and build the exterior walls of your home right now. A majority of tiny homes are built of wood cladding (timber weatherboards) since they are less expensive and appear more attractive for a smaller home. For this, you'll need an experienced carpenter, or if you believe you could do it yourself , then go ahead but ensure that you do not waste in time or money that you can earn with an existing job.

Another extremely useful item to put on your tiny house is a tank-water service which collects all rainwater off your roof.

You can put it on the outside of your home now, after the exterior cladding has been completed and your house is completely weatherproof.

Lock up stage

The stage lock up is a combination of tasks to prepare the frame to be plastered.

This includes:

Engaging an electrician to begin the wiring. Often referred to as a "rough-in" this is when they cut holes into your framework and connect all the wires that will be connected later during the building. I suggest hiring an electrician.

Inviting a plumber to begin the plumbing. Also called a "rough-in which is the time to make holes in the frame and run all the pipes that are ready to be fitted later on in the construction. I suggest hiring an experienced plumber.

Straightening walls by using straight edges as well as timber packers and a planer to rid of any bumps on the walls made of timber. For plaster to flow onto the walls without bumps.

Insulate the ceiling and walls to minimize heat loss and in retaining the hot or cool air inside your home.

The installation of stairs is a must if there are stairs and you live in an a triple or double story house

Plastering stage

When everything is prepared to be plastered, we can place an order and then hang the plaster. This is a simple task which we can all complete by ourselves. It's all you need is a companion or two along with a screw gun like the ones plasterers employ.

For the process of plastering, all you need to do is to look at a few YouTube videos YouTube to get a better understanding of how to go about it. You'll be able to place the plaster sheets on the ceiling and walls yourself if you're physically fit person. However, to achieve professional results, I would suggest hiring a plasterer to finish the 'stopping upwards' (getting rid of the joints that are in the walls).

Lockups: Fit off and fix Stage

The fitting off stage can be simply described as connecting all plumbing and electrical services and then finishing the final phases of carpentry. In this stage, you'll have just completed all of the above. Your carpenter will build any doors or skirtings, architraves, cabinets or cupboards.

Painting:

We're now ready for the most enjoyable aspect of art. It's all about finding the colors you love and then making sure that you smooth and brush the entire thing equally. Painting isn't that difficult and it's very relaxing, however it's definitely a skill to make everything perfectly neat and tidy when it comes on the precise line. It is important to concentrate on making sure that everything is neat while doing it and apply long, smooth strokes that are all in the same direction. The best method to paint is to paint up and down the walls, but not right and left horizontally since the paint could be drawn downwards. Also , make sure to apply painter's masking tape on doors and windows where you are not planning to paint.

Flooring:

Once all the tedious tasks are completed it's time to put in the flooring we'd like. Based on whether you'd like tiles flooring, carpet or floor boards, I would suggest hiring a tradesperson for the job unless you are able to demonstrate the expertise and skills to complete the task yourself.

Finishing:

We now complete the steps necessary to finish the building. We now install all of the door handles, door stops and appliances, as well as the kitchen stove tops, folding beds, and drawers that are hidden beneath stairs cases (anything that adds an accent). Usually, staining floors and the installation of carpet are the two last important step.

Then you'll be living in a tiny home designed to fit your specific design that is sustainable and self-sufficient.

Carpentry and Building advice:

Be aware throughout the entire construction if you are able to purchase the necessary materials and have them delivered to the your site, you'll save at most 15% on your build. This is because most builders will include a mark-up of 10-15% on the materials. If you're interested, you'll also be attending auctions for builders to purchase cheap materials that were left over from others' jobs or not placed orders for. If you're looking for the concept of saving money, then this is a great idea to take your time to search for online where the closest auctions for builders are, and then bidding on various items that you'll need to complete your work. You could end up savings of up to 15%!!

Chapter 14: Renovate, Reorganize and Celebrate!

In this case, one must begin with the feeling of your own heart of renovating because it is the first true step towards changing. If you are first introduced to the idea of altering the style of your home according to your personal size, color and taste You should dive into it!

Your small but significant micro-living is creating an enormous profit on the world's carbon footprints every minute. Always leave room for an additional guests, family members and belongings to ensure that your comfort is maintained as well as mobile. Start by opening every area of your home, microscopically.

Renovate and relax

Guidelines:

A highly therapeutic method that helps you get rid of anger and apathy, the act of renovating helps to relax and unwind. Let's begin with the fundamentals of renovation:

Choose your house!

You can also do the project and then, eventually, give your home a name! Choose a lovely word that describes you and your family members who reside at the home. You can also draw something. Or Scribble. You can also write. Whatever you choose to do you do, give your house an address!

Create your entry, specific and concise:

This is about the physical entrance to the home. Most of the time, we find that the entrance to the house is grand unneeded and a waste of space and all the little house is viewed from behind. To resolve this issue, keep your entrance brief, easy and classy. The entrance of your house is not a time to delay or hinder the flow of traffic at your house. There should be space to store Coat rack or shoe rack, as well as other essential amenities for guests to use. Your entrance space could hold mobile furniture, movable shelves or cabinets as well!

Create a dazzling and imaginative design of relaxation and then stay there: Make your space a place of concentration, peace and calm. Consider the space, visualize it in your mind, and decorate it. You can relax in your renovated area and design your own cozy area to relax and unwind!

Create a private "tripping space," filled with lights, sounds and art. Whatever your space might be whether it's a flat, room or bungalow, be sure to discover your own private space. Space for private space does not have to be a private space at the end of your room, it could be in the middle of the room that is decorated with a glow-in-the-dark lighting system and pendent images hanging from the ceiling. Create a ambiance with sound and lighting. The possibilities of lighting your private space to be illuminated with optical fibers will require the least amount of expenditure, right now. All you need is some optical fibres and the torch!

Resize:

The most important aspect of renovating involves changing the size of your home. In the process of transforming your vast expanse into cabinets and a wildly inventive doses of reality you're able to step in and out of an feeling of intimacy. This keeps you at line with gravity. Resize makes you think of your home as a nest, and even as a house.

Space-saving storage that is healthy and safe:

Make more storage space by changing your basements and berths. Make sure you have a clean and healthy area when creating your storage space. Storage must be warm and breathable throughout the day. Many people also grow bunnies, plants and vegetables within their cellar storage within controlled areas!

Kitchen efficiency:

The kitchen is a place of cleanliness, taste and deliciousness. As a place of worship to cook, the kitchen demands you to be extremely careful when it comes time to redesign and re-designing. A well-designed kitchen is a functional kitchen! Cover it with a sheet, keep it safe and keep it tidy!

Peace and Leisure:

To ensure relaxation and peace it is essential to always adjust the size in the context of comfort at the top of the head. The kitchen must always have room for items like tables chairs, a table and other "stuff" to ensure that it is all set and planned. Look online for kitchen window herbs to keep everything well-hydrated and free of cockroaches!

Reorganise and rejuvenate

Tricks

Create more space by dividing it into smaller sections.

Create a stunning passageway in the process of rearranging hallways

The light is the most important thing. Go online to find ways to create amazing DIY lighting at your home!

Put glass in anything or everything in your home. Mirrors windows, window, collectibles ceramics, and artefacts are all beautiful alternatives available to increase the value of your home as your home! Make a few hundred dollars and make the right investment, and you will be rewarded with stunning.

Ceiling Art: the central feature of a house and room Ceiling art is an amazing idea for imaginative minds that are out there! It will shine in the dark with the pendent light walls, partitions, cupboards music and lights can make it an absolute blast!

Allow furniture to breathe. All furniture must be placed in a space that is not too close with the wall. They should breathe at all times. Maintain them in a central position and not too close to walls. Create wall hangings and cabinets for those who require an intimate relationship with your space. Be sure your furniture inspires you!

Don't cover windows to create a space of comfort, you can leave your windows unadorned or covered in transparent objects. The windows are your eyes as well as the the soul of a house. Maintain them in a straight and central position to ensure that the living area is spacious.

The creation of a laundry room, drying area or washing room at home is essential.

Remove the Stairsor remove the Stairsor add stairs to your home.

Your budget is your best companion, friend and enemy. Make sure that you breathe in it after you have everything in place!

Chapter 15: Deciding to Living In A

Small House

There are many reasons this Tiny House Movement has become all the rage in current times. It inspires us with an idea that started with early settlers in the New World. They had a house they could build for by themselves and then take wherever they traveled.

No matter if you're living by yourself or a couple or retired There's plenty to gain by having a less stressful lifestyle. Take a look at these numbers regarding living in a smaller space.

55% of people who live in tiny homes have savings accounts that are larger.

78% of the people own their tiny home for themselves, which means there is no mortgage payment.

The cost of tiny homes is $23,000, while it is more than $272,000 for traditional homes.

The typical tiny house is 182 sq. feet. as opposed to 2100 sq. feet. for a traditional home.

Eighty percent of small home owners have lower credit card debt than the mean and 65% of them have no debt.

Although these are all fantastic advantages to investing in a tiny home but they're not the only reason to opt for a tiny house. If you look at the average price of a typical home with a tiny one and you can easily appreciate the financial benefits by going small.

A Conscious Decision

Although money is among the primary reasons for investing in a tiny home, it isn't the only reason. The majority of people don't take small homes lightly. Once they've gotten the facts there are many who feel the need to be a part of an environmentally responsible and socially responsible decision.

Carbon Footprint

In a world in which waste is among the most significant offenses you can do to the environmental and the fact that small dwellings can significantly reduce carbon emissions is a huge benefit. The fact that we are destroying all of the resources that we have at a fast rate proves that the small house movement is just in time. Some experts go further and saying the resources we have are getting exhausted faster than we can replenish them.

If you take into account the environmental impact of the construction of a traditional house the savings can be staggering. For a typical home, you'll require about 16000 board feet wood as well as another 14,000 square. feet. of wood products for the project. It's around seven fully loaded logging trucks for one home. Additionally, you'll require concrete, petroleum-based products and metals as well as other building materials, in addition to the energy required to construct the home. As a comparison, the materials required for a tiny house are just a tiny portion of that.

Great Retirement Home

For empty nesters who want to reduce their size and simplify their lives, tiny houses are great retirement residences. For every tiny home owner approximately 40% are above 50. This lets seniors enjoy a comfortable life on a fixed salary and also limits their space required for a comfortable life for the majority of them. Furthermore, because the majority of tiny houses can be mobile and quickly moved to more suitable places, it is possible to be near or live with their adult children without needing the need to "live with" their children, which is an ideal solution for all parties.

A Tiny House: Pros and Cons tiny House

There's no doubt that the appeal of tiny homes is quickly growing. With increasing numbers of people fall to the costs of traditional homes and their maintenance costs, the necessity to streamline their lives through smaller homes is becoming an essential as well as with the environmental impact that larger homes are placing on the environment, tiny homes are the best option. There are advantages and disadvantages to this kind of lifestyle and it's worthwhile to look at these elements to ensure that you can afford a small house the next option for you.

The Benefits

The contemporary style of tiny houses are not just playhouses that have been remodeled for adults. They are completely equipped with everything that you need in a bigger house. Naturally, the tiny home you pick will be designed for your lifestyle however, you can expect to have everything from basic necessities to the modern life with all of the modern amenities.

Of course, many homeowners opt for tiny homes due to their simple life style. They are simple to personalize with furniture which can give every area of the home additional function.

The disadvantages

However, the reality is that tiny homes aren't for everyone. It requires a certain kind of person to have a smaller home. Prior to the beginning of the planning stage of your tiny house you'll need to think differently. It is essential to maximize every square inch and any other addition you're considering should have multiple purposes.

The location of the house is also an important issue. A lot of tiny homes are designed to be mobile and you'll need to consider how to move it. If you're planning on mobility it will require the aid of a trailer and truck for moving it around. If you're planning to build an all-time fixed residence There are legal concerns to think about regarding where you're permitted to construct.

Tiny homes are most popular among singles. And as more individuals you bring into the tiny area the more friction you cause. The sharing of space in these tiny homes can be a challenge. It can be difficult to maintain privacy when you want it, unless you've already thought of it.

Due to limited space due to the limited space, you'll need to make more trips to complete the errands. There won't be a conventional size fridge that can store food items If you're not into gardening or canning then you're likely to find that you'll be unable to buy many items, which means additional shopping trips.

The most likely drawback for living in a tiny house is weather. Sure, you can construct your tiny home with all the insulation required to withstand extreme temperatures, however tiny houses are an issue in areas with high winds and areas susceptible to fires. There have been instances where entire houses were taken. Also, it is important to think about the possibility that insuring your home's value might not be as simple as purchasing homeowner's insurance. It could result in an enormous liability should anything transpire in the future.

If you're used being in large house , it can be hard to imagine living living in a tiny home. If you're among those fortunate few who can benefit from the advantages and overcome the negatives and draw the best benefits, you're in for truly enjoyable experience. You'll not only have more money, time, and less distractions, but you'll also be able to enjoy a better, simpler level of quality life.

As Baby Boomers enter retirement and Millennials face the problems of the present property market, lots of people are considering consideration to the Tiny House Movement serious consideration.

Chapter 16: The Changes in Lifestyle:

How to Deal With It

Tiny homes have their own style of living. Moving to a different home isn't always easy, because it takes time for people to adjust to any changes in their lives. We will address what you can expect to change as you move to smaller space and how you can deal with these changes.

It is advisable to move to a small house that meets your standards and needs. This is an effective way to help you adjust to the new environment easily since you will be more at ease in a situation that you don't feel uncomfortable.

Lifestyle change and the best way to manage these changes:

Changes in lifestyles can be a reason for a subsidised and more simple life. It may not appear to be an enormous change, however, in reality it's quite different. The bigger houses offer plenty of space, whether you wish to wander around, or store your belongings. With less space it is necessary to adjust in a less crowded way.

However, it may result in different activities. You could try running instead of staying inside the daytime, leading to positive outcomes.

A smaller house will drastically reduce the amount of work within the home or the responsibilities you have, so that you will have less space to maintain and clean. Thus, it leads to more time to relax like previously. You can choose to be content with the extra time you can spend with take for yourself today. For others, it could be a bit boring or frustrating to be in a state of relaxation.

In this situation, you may decide to engage engaging in other healthful activities based on your own personal preferences. The practice of yoga is generally healthy exercise that helps to improve the peace of mind and the body. You can also participate in your preferred sport, cook or bake or meet with your friends, etc.

The best method to adapt is to prepare yourself in advance. This could be done by going to various tiny homes or meeting the people who live there. Going to them will provide a glimpse of what it's going to be for you. Also, meeting other people can help you gain from their experiences and understanding what it's like to reside in such a setting. It is important to be prepared in order to prepare yourself mentally for the changes.

In fact, it could be an excellent thing to consider doing this before you decide to move to a smaller home, as it is impossible to make a change.

How can you be creative with your tiny home:

*Innovation is born from this. The most important factor is to be a passionate about your work and everything you do. This lets you fully be absorbed in the work that you have to complete and to be at your very best.

In the beginning, you should start by brainstorming ideas that pop into your head in regards to what you would like to see inside your tiny home.

Next step, you must analyze. The next step is to determine the essentials and what's not. You can also create an additional list in the list of non-essential items you'd want to include.

The next step is to think about the viability of the ideas you've recorded till you've got a complete list of options. However, you must take your time to ensure that you have the time to think through all possible options rather than just doing some one-time brainstorming.

The next step is to think of new ideas. It is important to consider including them all into your home without looking too crowded or crowded. You can make shelving and separators, containers or foldable furniture. This kind of furniture allows you to be flexible by being able to reduce size as required to decrease the visual impact and prevent your home from appearing too crowded. You can even engage an expert home decorator to help you through the furniture if you wish.

The next step is to review the list of luxury items you would like to include in your home. You could make your own ideas or employ an expert to help you in the right direction.

If it is a construction project or renovation, you could employ an architect from the beginning. It is important to note that the design of the home can impact the way it appears and the use of space can be affected by the style. One example is that you could create walls that separate to create distinct shapes that will help you clearly define and divide each room.

It is possible to choose an escalator or a double storey home if you require additional space. However, it has to be connected to the foundation of the home so that it can be able to support a larger structure.

What should you do to move or not to a tiny home?

The decisions you make should be based on logic. First, you must determine if you enjoy the idea of tiny homes or not. When more than one person participates, viewpoints of each must be weighedor thought about.

You must then decide the reasons why you would like to move to a smaller home and you do not think you would like it. It is possible that you like something, but do not would you want to own it. This is why it is crucial to establish a clear line. As mentioned earlier you might want to meet with people living in tiny homes and ask them about how it feels like or go to various homes yourself to get an impression of the houses to aid in making an informed decision.

You have to decide on your budget and what you would like to invest in your house. With that in mind, you have to determine what is the best deal for you.

Chapter 17: Easiest Home

Organization Hacks

Keeping your home organized is a surefire method of getting rid of clutter and saving space. In this article you'll discover the most effective ways to manage even the most basic things within your home. The best part is that you don't need to purchase everything! Materials are easily accessible at your home.

Use shoeboxes to divide your cabinet

It's great that when a pair of shoes are taken out of the box, it is taken straight to your dependable shoe rack. So you'll be able to view them and choose them when you require them. What happens to the boxes?

Don't throw themaway! They can be used as cabinet dividers to separate a variety of different items. For instance, you can divide your underwear!

Rain gutter as floating bookshelf

The majority of homeowners alter their gutters every now and then and if it's is the right time to spend with your family Don't be tempted to clean out the rain gutters too quickly You can make use of them as shelves that can be used to store books, other small knick-knacks and more. This doesn't mean you don't have to do anything however all you have be able to paint is in the hue that matches your decor and then put them on your walls.

Ice cube tray is a jewelry organizer (or there's also the palette)

Are you bored of constantly searching for your jewelry, specifically the tiniest earrings? You don't need to buy an accessories organizers, your own freezer tray will work perfectly. In this task it's easy to make you have to do. Just arrange your jewellery on the tray of ice cubes and voila! If you don't have a tray is available, you could also use the palette to paint.

Paper for the toilet to secure your cords

Another method you can do at home is to organize your cords with toilet tube made of paper. Simply roll the cords, then place them inside the tube. After that, you can you can label them.

Flip table for children

Flipping the desk for children is possibly the best ideas for saving space you could use for an idea for a project. It's not as easy as the other organizational hacks, but it does not mean you won't encounter difficulties. This is a project that's both simple and rewarding.

The top things that create chaos and the best way to eliminate these issues!

The smallest of things are often the most difficult to manage Most times these are the things that create chaos within your home. Find out how you can organize the clutter using these simple steps:

Assorted knick-knacks station

What should be included What to include: Matches, sunglasses lighting bulbs, candles tools measuring tape, matches, and other things you don't use often but can come in handy on events. To store these items it is only necessary to have one level of a moderate-sized pull-out cabinet.

Tips:

As much as you can you can, classify the items by similarity. Examples include items from the toolbox matchboxes, candles and so on.

*For maximum space, you can use a cut-to-fit mat made of rubber as partitions.

Paper Station

This station is a must for parents of children. If they can't be able to have their own study space due to absence of space, they should at least have a writing station. To arrange this station you'll need a tiny shelf that is ideally three levels.

What should be included What to include: writing materials, coupons bonds, test papers Invitation, or other important documents.

Tips:

You can choose to have an adjustable shelf so that you can increase or lower the height to suit your needs.

* Sort papers according to the purpose they serve such as for projects, artwork, for scratch and more.

*To make space Label the documents in accordance with their owner.

Set up a bulletin board on which you can place announcements, invitations as well as other agendas. It also serves as a useful reminder of what you can eliminate.

*At the lowest point of the shelf include a large open box that kids are able to "pass" their exam paper.

And lastly, get shredder. This will help you stop conserving documents you no longer require.

The electronic-Station

Electrical appliances can turn into clutter. It's an excellent idea to organize these things and put them in only one location.

What you should include What should be included? Charger cords, earphones charger, batteries, adapter remote control, electrical tape. Like the Knick-knacks Assorted Station you'll need the pullout level of a drawer to organize this.

Tips:

Use cut-to-fit rubber to create dividers to create shelves. They can be adjusted, and flexible, making them ideal to make the most of space.

Have a few clamps available to help tidy the cords.

For smaller items such as watches' batteries, keep them in a

One Stop Craft Station

Another great station to set up is a crafting station ideal for families who have an creative talents and who enjoy DIY projects. Make use of a shelf to organize this area.

What should be included Include: Wrapping materials, ribbons cards, tapes scrapbooking items, glue including scissors, crayons and markers

TIPS:

Use rods to hang gifts wrappers.

Jars can be used to organize small scrapbooking items. To make space, place the jars to the bottom of the shelves.

*For ribbons, utilize paper towels as holders.

* Place the crayons and markers in bigger containers , so children can see the colors they require right away.

Best 20 Room Saving Furniture

Doc Sofa Bed

This Doc Sofa Bed is a single-unit sofa-to-bunkbed converter that comes with a removable fabric that is washable and reusable cover, and a fully-slatted wood base for extra stability. This comfortable and versatile piece is an architectural work of art that will leave you amazed by the space you'll get. The ladder that is simple to put together serves as a sturdy and sturdy scaffolding for the sofa that can be converted into furniture for bedding.

Fold down Table

This wall-mounted chalkboard folds down into an ideal single-person work space that is easy to assemble and disassembly. The flip-up table is perfect to work on crafts or sewing DIY projects. It is also great for homework for the college student with a limited space. The frame is customizable and can accommodate images, artwork, and any other innovative ideas you might want to put along the border to personalize this space-saving device! The tabletop is two-in-one and includes chalkboard, chalkboard storage compartments, an eraser as well as useful hanging hardware for easy assembly.

Hollow Chair

The sophisticated and fun design for a chair created by Judson Beaumont will have even the most cluttered of people wondering how they can fit in the undercarriage that is this loveseat. Its "hollow" design (hence its name) lets you easily and customized storage, making this chair your own personal throne! It is filled with toys for children as well as books for those who love reading yoga mats, water bottles for the home fitness enthusiast and many more individual items.

Knife-within-a-Knife

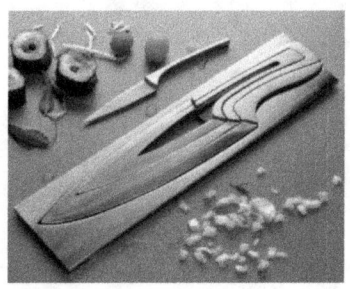

This unique knife set is different from any other set of knives you'll ever own! It's a sturdy piece of culinary art that'll leave one wondering exactly where the space-saving set was all your life! This modern Mia Schmallenbach cutlery set made of stainless steel with high-quality blades, is available in an all-in-one block. The Deglon Meeting Knife set, designed in France comes with an a 3-1/4-inch pairing knife inside a 5-1/4 inch utility knife that is encased in an 8-inch chef knife inside an 8-3/4 inch slicer and each set is nestled inside the stainless steel block that matches.

Convertible Sofa

The modern convertible sofa provides an inviting and relaxing space that can be used for the use of a compact and robust multi-functional. In the present day of smaller living spaces the convenience factor is among the primary considerations when considering the type of style you'd like to convey in your home. This luxurious and comfortable piece of art can be transformed from a couch with a variety of colors to a stunning Oakwood table that has mini-chairs. The cushion cushions can be removed to give the possibility of mixing and matching colors, as well as additional seating should floor seating be required, and also allows for simple storage. This versatile piece is ideal for people who have limited space or preference for minimalist furniture.

Ironing Board Mirror

Have you ever wished for an all-length mirror that didn't take the space of your home or sagging against the wall? This Ironing Board Mirror is just the perfect solution! This ironing board comes with the stability required to iron your favourite garment or dress, as well as providing you with the full-length mirror you require to appreciate how gorgeous you appear. The small size of the mirror and ironing board combination allows for simple storage and use even in the tiniest of spaces.

The Dining Room Table, Chairs and Table

The dining chairs is popular for when you're having guests or family members to join you for a casual brunch or even a small gathering in your small home. If the chairs are placed set in the center of this table whole structure is able to be used as kind of 'middle room' coaster or ottoman. The table offers plenty of leg space underneath and the chairs are built to help support the back and the central part of the person seated in this beautiful dining set. After the chairs have been taken away and the table is set, it transforms into a stunning and appealing table that can seat four of your best family and friends.

Stair Drawers

These staircases are among the most inventive storage solutions! The standard staircases provide support and stability needed to move from one level of your home to the next. However, with the stair drawers think of the things you don't need to take the stairs to get. These stairs drawers as toys for your children, extra storage for cleaning up, or compact vacuum sets and provide easy access to extra space to store things that would not require a place other than an area that is out of view and hidden from view. However, an word of caution...ensure that each drawer is shut by closing it before taking the next step!

Bookcase Stairwell

Imagine being in a hallway that is populated with novels by the most famous authors of all time? Imagine being able to choose the latest novel to devour as you head to the kitchen for a cup of morning coffee? Genius! This bookcase staircase is definitely an interesting conversation piece! While the bookcase stairwell designed to make use of the empty space on the hallway wall by creating the appearance of a bookcase however, the attraction of having a completely different view of what a typical hallway is will leave your guests wondering whether it would be an ideal feature for their house too!

Open-and-Close Barbeque

Do you enjoy grilling outside? Do you or anyone else you know have a large barbecue grill? Do you want more space in your backyard to relax and enjoy your outdoor space? This set of open and closed barbeque will be stylish and offer you the space you require to unwind by the pool. The black metallized steel grilling set includes grilling plate as well as cooking utensils. The wall mount for outdoor use is compact and can be easily tucked away to make a an easy and space-saving piece of furniture that is certain to impress your party guests.

Roel Verhagen-Kaptein Three in One

The multi-functional design of this chair can fill even the most cramped of spaces open to options. The chair can transform from a single seat an intimate seat to a three-person sofa in a matter of minutes. It's even the equivalent of a mini-sofa bed in case unexpected guests are invited to stay at your new, chic home. The combination of comfort and technology comes together in this functional, yet sturdy piece of furniture, designed by the interior designer Roel Verhagen-Kaptein. This chair is certainly one for the books , and one you can trust to offer the highest level of ease of use and flexibility.

Dror in order to Pick Chair

If you're deciding between furniture and wall art take a look at the chic combination of both in the Pick Chair by Dror. If you think of folding chairs they are a space-saving option. benefit to their lack of style and style. With its innovative mix of function and art the furniture will surely fulfill your desires for class and function. This Pick Chair comes in a polished wood finish. One side features a tree image etched on it, while the other features an image of a smaller tree saw sketched on its back. These simple but visually appealing images provide the furniture with an aesthetic. It's a shame to miss out on a fantastic furniture piece that will save space if you don't get these stunning panels of comfortable seating.

Foldable Swiss Bookshelf

Moving day is often the most difficult. The boxes are stacked at the top of the stairs, the entire collection your precious items being handled, transported from the place to another- it's exhausting just to think about it! The most difficult items to relocate are the bulky and large ones such as bookcases and couches. Now, the stress caused by the former is gone! The bookcase that folds up was designed to be lightweight and looks cool while doing it! It was designed in the hands of Swiss interior designer Kurt Thut, this furniture product is a great way to records that you put on your bookcase that folds... The shelves shrinks to the lower shelf and all you're remaining with is a foundation of shelves that can better fit in that tiny space that you have between the boxes of kitchenware and bathroom decor.

One Shot Stool

This stool is a cool...seat! It may appear small, but this clever chair folds up and unfolds to create one of the most impressive examples of minimalist seating that I've ever seen. The folding chairs typically be more bulky than they can save However, this One-Shot Stool eliminates the bulk and rigidity of even the smallest of folding chair. The design was created by the Belgian furniture company Materialise.MGX The folding stool eliminates those problems. It's one hand to fold this chair down into a seating option and then a simple turn in the palm to close it. When closed The One Shot Stool is no bigger than the stick one would find in the outdoors, providing mobility and flexibility to become a leading contender in the race for the most comfortable and most imaginative design for chairs.

LunaBlocks Lego Furniture

This huge version of the childhood classic, Legos, could make even the most miserable of your friends smile as they remember fond moments of playing time! These imaginative and fun pieces of furniture are actually able to fit the other, just like real-sized Legos to make it easy to put together and removal. The most appealing aspect of this adorable piece is that after the dinner gathering (or the tea hour!) is finished, putting them in a stack is simple!

Fix it on the wall furniture

Have you ever thought of putting up your dining table to create extra space? Have you ever wanted a modern art on your wall but didn't know which wall to place it on? Then this dining set is able to serve as a modern wall art while saving space! This is the perfect combination! The furniture piece, created by John Nouanesing, is available in a variety of textures and colors as well as prints. It has plugs that are removable to fit even the tiniest of rooms.

It's a four-chair tea-style set that will impress your guests from setting up until the time it is taken down!

Fusion of a Pool Table, Dining Table as well as a Table

This mix of fun and eating is perfect for the bachelor or bachelorette house that might require more space than large tables. Each table was built in Belgium by the furniture designer firm Aramith and is available in four different finishes (Dark Oak Wenge, Walnut, Grey Oak as well as Light Oak) to suit the individual's preferences and tastes. The table also comes with Simonis the 760-inch poolcloth, as well as the dining table top is included. This table is affordable and offers more of a full-sized game table for the modern dining space!

Kenchikukagu Fold Out Apartment Set

Have you ever witnessed an entire apartment utility set rolled from a single box? No! It's but not for a while! This Fold-Out Apartment Set by Kenchikukagu features simple design, but with the appearance of baroque to the design. This furniture set costs $7500. It comprises three cabinets that fold up to an open kitchen space with an open drawer that can be pulled out and folded out counter, and an office area that has drawers and shelf space and bedrooms with an a small counter-top and an overhead shelf for a simple reading area. The set comes with wheels that allow for mobility and can easily fit in your closet to store things in the event of need.

Casulo

Have you ever wanted furniture that you could easily pack up and move around with ease? Do you wish you had an area that can accommodate everything at your workplace? Take a look at the Casulo set that is all-in-one for your apartment that was designed by Marcel Kings & Sebastian Muhlhauser It is available in a bright yellow square to brighten the space. This piece of furniture is innovative and can be arranged to make an living room set. The compact storage unit includes three stools, a desk and a bookcase with six shelves, an armoire, and the bed! Plus is that the mattress can fit inside too and can be removed and reassembled within a matter of minutes, without the use of tools.

Sleeping in

In conclusion, I'm going to declare that I've saved the top for the last! This is certainly the most efficient and ingenuous piece of furniture we have on our list! It's basically a flying bed...not necessarily, but it's at least as close as you can be! This Bed Up is perfect for loft owners or studio tenant who's severely lacking space but is still looking for the most stylish. This design reminds us of the 1980's wall bed which folded down the wall using a lift off the top. The Bed Up has been improved and gives the most innovative and originality. The bed-to-ceiling furniture can save you about 30 square feet of space in any space, and it slides into place when not being used. Another feature that could add to the stylish and fashionable bed is the lighting beneath it to save even more space by utilising it as a light in the bedroom too!

Chapter 18: Different Types of Tiny

Houses.

With tiny houses being built all over the nation, no one would find it surprising to hear people talk about the desire of people to "go smaller." Everyone is on the lookout to cut costs, decrease carbon footprints and discover how it feels living in a smaller space.

It is, however, much more complicated to purchase or construct tiny space. Many factors have to be considered, including the life style of the inmates as well as the construction process that must be carried out. Additionally it is a nationwide event that not everyone can take part in.

Here are ten crucial questions every homeowner should ask before deciding whether or not to purchase a tiny home:

There'll be significant costs to be paid in advance, therefore do you have the funds to save?

Building a smaller home is a big obstacle. Are you prepared for it?

A tiny home could take an entire year, or even two. So are you prepared to sit and wait?

Imagine a garage that is just one car. Would you be capable of living in a smaller area than this?

Do you think it's okay that you have to wear only the one shoe?

Do you have a space for parking it? An asphalt driveway can suffice, however you'll need to have one!

Sharing resources is the most efficient way to live in a small space. Do you want to share your resources?

A few tiny homes include bathrooms while other don't. Are you comfortable with answering Nature's call in a variety of ways?

Are you living a life that is suited to the constraints to living within a small home?

Does your home represent more than the four walls and the roof?

Tiny homes come in various types however, they generally be classified into two categories: non-moveable and moveable. A tiny home that can be moved is built on wheels, whereas an unmoveable one is built on the foundation.

Traveling Tiny Homes

There are actually three kinds of tiny houses that you could live in. Only one is considered to be a "true" tiny house that is based on its exterior and the interior. It is important to note that all three choices would be considered to be RV living.

Trailer Tiny Home

This is the classic tiny home , which has become an iconic "fad" that is trending in the millennium. The tiny home of this style is constructed with frames made of metal or wood and siding for a regular home and a shingled or metal roof, and is outfitted with your ideal home. for it. Start from scratch and build a house that is attractive from an architectural standpoint, and also is able to be mounted on a trailer at least 65 feet maximum, which includes that tow vehicle.

Converted Bus

Commercial and school buses have been converted to turn them into tiny homes to provide cheap living. There are buses that are and set up to allow living in an RV. Music groups usually use buses for travel, however they are expensive. There are a few individuals who bought used transport buses, taken out the seats, windowsand windows and constructed a tiny home inside. They've created it to look like a house inside rather than the RV style of the majority of travel buses.

RVs

Motorhomes and RVs aren't homes at all. They're made for camping , not a permanent home. This doesn't mean that you cannot stay in a motorhome all the time. A lot of them have been used for years as part of fairs, circuses and other festivals. But, they're equipped more to be used for camping, including the camping-style beds as well as bathrooms and kitchens. You can also purchase an old RV, take it apart and make it into a small home, with granite countertops and a larger vertical wall and better storage ideas.

Non-Moveable Tiny Houses

Anyone can design your dream home which is less than a typical house. It will be constructed on a foundation and built according to your requirements. But, there's an alternative to the traditional wood frame home you can select as a home that isn't moveable.

You can build an "container" for your home. You can find shipping containers that range from $1,000 to $6,000. You can then get windows and doors cut out of the steel, and frames that are welded to the windows and doors and then alter the interior of the container to make your own tiny home. This type of construction is very well-liked in coastal cities with shipyards. You can purchase one-use containers. That means that they've traveled the sea in one direction or round trip.

Container houses are very popular in states that are prone to hurricanes. The steel construction of containers make it hard for the house to be damaged during an event of hurricane, in particular, when the doors made of steel are kept on to guard the main entrance to the house.

Chapter 19: The Benefits Of Tiny Houses

For some thinking of living in a small space may appear to be a bizarre idea however, it seems to be taking off. There is a growing interest in creating their own tiny homes; there's a so-called "tiny home movement" which is spreading across the country.

These people would not be able to live this kind of life if there were no advantages to having a smaller home.

A tiny home basically requires you to undergo an entirely new perspective on the way you live and the choices you make on an every day basis.

We live in a heavily capitalized time in which an accumulation of huge amounts of stuff that is useless is supported.

A tiny home alters this. It's not possible to buy things all the time since you'd be wasting the space you have in your small dwelling in the event that you did.

The tiny space will also help reduce the carbon footprint. The tiny home requires less energy to operate. It will only require at most 2 bulbs to illuminate the entire home. You can heat your home with the stove that is small and will require a smaller capacity air conditioner when the weather gets too hot.

The lower the amount of resources you utilize in your home, the more beneficial it is to the environment. If you record the environmental-friendly measures you take each day and you'll find that you've actually reduced your carbon footprint significantly when compared to living in a standard home.

A majority of tiny houses are placed upon tops of trailers, allowing to move around more easily. Simply tying your trailer to the tow vehicle will allow you to move across vast distances.

That means that should you have to travel to another state, you shouldn't have any issues finding the right place to stay when you take your home with you.

The additional mobility frees you from having to put a large importance on working in a single location. There is no need to fret about having to leave your home due to work opportunities elsewhere. Just move your home to that location.

You should engage someone to construct your project for you?

A tiny house, as every other structure in the residential sector, must be built with the utmost precision. There's no room to make errors while building a small home. A structural flaw could result in the house to collapse and cause injury to anyone who is near or in the tiny home. A tiny home is also exposed to pressure when it is moved from one area to one location to. If you are able to cut corners when building this will surely reduce the structural strength of your house.

This is a total loss of money.

If you're not confident with your carpentry abilities, you should get someone else to build the tiny home for you. This will ultimately mean you'll add the expense of labor to your construction budget. However, there's no value to be placed on your and other people's safety.

It is also possible to help in building your home to reduce cost of labor. It means that you'll need help out and work hard. The savings you can get by choosing this option is not significant, but the knowledge gained by working on your tiny home is invaluable.

The more effort you put into the tiny home the more experience you'll acquire. Being aware of the inside functioning of your tiny home can be extremely helpful when you're required to do any future repairs.

Another great benefit of small-sized house communities: home owners are always ready to assist in the construction of the perfect tiny home. Make sure you are part within the small home community in your region so you'll have people to lend a hand when you're working on your project. You will not only make new friends by this method but you'll also avoid the mistakes that commonly happen to first-time builders when building their tiny homes.

Take part in lectures, seminars or even workshops on tiny-house lifestyle to gain the best tips and tricks to build tiny homes. This is also a fantastic method to connect with other people and to find the most cost-effective construction companies or the most cost-effective materials that are available on the market.

Chapter 20: Tiny House Design

Essentials - Interior

A tiny home is different from the typical home. It is designed so that every space is utilized. A tiny home's design is restricted by space and dictated by the needs of the homeowners. This is the reason the design of a tiny home can be more difficult than a typical home. This chapter will explore the essential aspects of design for tiny homes.

Furniture

Lester Walker, the author of the very first tiny house book in 1960, coined the term"furniture," which is a reference to furniture that can be turned into another thing. For example the table can be transformed into a bed or couch when you go to bed at night with a few simple adjustments. Because tiny homes are limited in area, investing in furniture that's functional is a smart idea. Large furniture takes up much space in tiny homes. Here are some excellent design suggestions on how to select furniture that is functional for your small home:

Stackable Furniture

Selecting furniture that has many stacking options is crucial for those who live in small homes. Stackable furniture will make the most of every square inch within a tiny home. Furniture that can be stacked helps you free the space in your small home by arranging your furniture. A good example of furniture that is stackable includes chairs that can be stacked and untuck when you need to (during meals or breakfast).

Collapsible Furniture

Another kind of furniture that works for homes with small spaces is furniture that can be folded. Furniture that folds down is an excellent option to maximize space within your home because it lets you fold the furniture down to make the space you need in your home. For example, a dining table that can be collapsed can be easily moved to make more space for the kitchen on busy days.

Convertible furniture

One of the most essential furniture that you should purchase to furnish the home you live in are convertible furnishings. The name says it all the furniture can be transformed from the furniture you have in one form to another. For example the kitchen table could be used as a working station or bed based on the style. If you are looking to purchase convertible furniture for your small home Try to think of ways to make it work for you. For example, a dining tables in your kitchen could be used to create a workspace and also folds down to form a large bed for a sleeping area in the evening.

Functional furniture doesn't just help you make your small house more functional but also assist you to conserve space as well as the decor of your home.

Vertical Spaces

If you are designing a small house it is essential to make the most of all the space in your home. Utilizing vertical space is crucial to make sure that horizontal spaces are balanced inside your house. When you use the vertical space, you reduces the cluttered and claustrophobic feel of your home and also enhances the visuals from a vertical perspective inside small spaces. Here are some suggestions for using vertical spaces within your home to your advantage

To make use of vertical space You can make use of hooks, magnets and hooks and other organizational strategies. This is especially useful in organizing your small kitchen and bathroom. Hooks and magnets placed on walls lets you look at the items you typically use in these areas.

It is also possible to install fixtures that use vertical space within your home. For example creating a loft over the front of your home or even your kitchen is a fantastic method to make use of that space. There are shelves that you can install to make use of the vertical space as well as, in addition make use of the shelves to arrange your possessions or display unique trinkets to make your home an appearance.

Conclusion

The idea of moving to a smaller home is an excellent idea, but it's not something can be used by everyone. The key to making an effective transition is to make sure you're ready for the massive shift. It's not just about moving to an apartment that is smaller. It's a completely new way of life.

The preparation for your project includes researching and participating in the construction. This doesn't mean hitting a nail or installing a bolt, instead, being open about what you require and the way you'd like to plan the space. This will guarantee that when you're in the house the space, everything will be exactly just the way you intended the place to look.

It will assist you in determining the reason you want to go small. If it was another family member's suggestion, then knowing the details about living tiny will allow you to understand the ways it could benefit you.

It's also a good option to slowly transition. When you are waiting to move into your new house and begin to get used to living a more simple life by slowly adjusting your routine. A simple way to do this is to cut down on the television at night in the bedroom, and instead use your living room. It is also possible to reduce your wardrobe gradually so that you aren't shocked by the changes.

We hope this book given you all the information you require to know when making the choice to be small and how to adapt to the changes.

www.ingramcontent.com/pod-product-compliance
Lightning Source LLC
Chambersburg PA
CBHW071843080526
44589CB00012B/1090